The Spiritual General Manual Of Life

The Spiritual General Manual Of Life

KING SOLOMON SPIRITUAL LIBRARY
THE GOD ENCYCLOPAEDIA WORD OF INFINITY

BY
THE SPIRIT OF THE FATHER GOD
THROUGH HIS SERVANT
HRM KING SOLOMON DAVID JESSE ETE
(King Solomon Spiritual Library)
Eteroyal Universal Family BCS

All rights reserved
Copyright © Solomon ETE, 2008
Solomon ETE is hereby identified as author of this work in accordance with Section 77 of the Copyright, Designs and Patents Act 1988

The book cover picture is copyright to Solomon ETE

This book is published by
King Solomon Spiritual Library
P O BOX 27394
London E12 6WW UK
www.kingsolomonspirituallibrary.com

This book is sold subject to the conditions that it shall not, by way of trade or otherwise, be lent, resold, hired out or otherwise circulated without the author's or publisher's prior consent in any form of binding or cover other than that in which it is published and without a similar condition including this condition being imposed on the subsequent purchaser.

A CIP record for this book is available from the British Library

ISBN 978-0-9559801-5-2

Preface

As **I** always say, let every human heart be clean and clear and be with humility and with understanding with the love to hear from **THE FATHER GOD** once again. If you have that faith and belief then the communication between you and **I** will flow very well. But if you withhold your heart from **ME THE FATHER GOD** and hide yourself by having a double mind and doubting and not believing in **ME**, then the communication of understanding will be influenced by your thoughts as you do not believe **THE FATHER GOD**. That is the reason **I** bring all manners of information and all manners of explanations about **THE FATHER'S TALK (GOD PRESENT)**.

I want you to believe that **THE FATHER'S TALK (GOD PRESENT)** information is NOT motivated by cunning or by the human mind. It is NOT the WORD from the studio of carnality. It is NOT broadcasted by evil or by second thought of a human being. **THE FATHER'S TALK (GOD PRESENT)** information is a direct broadcast, straight from **THE FATHER GOD**. It is broadcasted directly from the studio of **THE FATHER GOD ALMIGHTY THE SUPREME WORD OF THE UNIVERSE**.

All **THE FATHER'S TALK (GOD PRESENT)** Lectures Revelations are direct from **THE FATHER GOD ALMIGHTY.** That is why **I** call this one **BEYOND THE HUMAN KNOW.**

When **I** exist **I** was, was, was and this information existed with **ME** and that means that indirectly, **THE FATHER GOD ALMIGHTY THE SUPREME WORD OF THE UNIVERSE** is revealing **HIMSELF** to humankind once again. **I** do this so that you would not continue to think that **THE FATHER GOD** does not speak with human beings directly anymore. And most importantly this **FATHER'S TALK (GOD PRESENT)** Lecture Revelations are NOT given via any angel. They are not inspirational outcome from one possessed by an angel or a ghost. They are directly from **THE FATHER GOD'S** possessing heart in that **I** TAKE OVER THE BODY, THE SOUL AND SPIRIT OF HRM KING SOLOMON DAVID JESSE ETE AND **I** TALK THROUGH HIM.

This book is title: ***The Spiritual General Manuals of Life* "THE ADMINISTRATOR"** as the key and **ENHANCEMENT** of the **GENERAL DIRECTIVE** and **MANUAL** to be used in governing the whole world.

Contents

Chapter One   **9-73**
The Manual Of The Spoken Word

Chapter Two   **75-150**
The Manual Of Life

Chapter Three   **151-218**
The Manual Of Investment With GOD

Chapter Four   **219-274**
Life Extension Manual

Chapter Five   **275-308**
Life Spiritual Fire Extinguisher Manual

Chapter Six   **309-351**
The Inspirational Writers

Chapter One

THE MANUAL OF THE SPOKEN WORD

(HOW TO SPEAK THE WORD)

The Spiritual General Manual Of Life

FATHER'S TALK
(GOD PRESENT)

Date: AO/AO/OG (The tenth day of the tenth month of **THE FATHER** 'year' two thousand and seven)

In the name of Our Lord Jesus Christ
In the blood of Our Lord Jesus Christ
Now and forever more, *Amien*

THE MANUAL OF THE SPOKEN WORD (HOW TO SPEAK THE WORD

The Word Is The Supreme Administrator Both In Heaven And On Earth And In The Spiritual, Physical And Otherwise.

THE WORD SEASON

Today is **AO** which is the tenth day of **THE WORD CELEBRATION SEASON** and **I AM** giving this Lecture Revelation to earmark this year's **WORD SEASON**. The Lecture Revelation that **I AM** going to give today is very **IMPORTANT** to all humans on earth, including the human **GOD**, human animals, human birds, and human fishes. Indeed any soul who has taken an **EVOLUTION** into this world as a human being must take this Lecture Revelation seriously.

First, no human being should disregard the **WORD** because **THE WORD IS THE SUPREME ADMINISTRATOR** both in heaven and on earth, and in the **SPIRITUAL**, **PHYSICAL** and **OTHERWISE**. The **SPIRIT** of **CHRIST** is the **SUPREME ADMINISTRATOR**. It is **THE SOLE SPIRITUAL HEAD**, the **CHRIST** of **GOD** and the **KING** of **KINGS** and the **LORD** of **LORDS**. It is **EVERYTHING** of **EVERYTHING**. It is the **MANIFESTOR**, the **CONVERTING MACHINE** of the **FATHER'S REALITY** as **REALSO** to

AMISO. **I** have used **MY LOVE, MY SUPREME HUMILITY, KINDNESS** and **MERCY** for humankind that **I** have created, in **MY IMAGE** and **LIKENESS**, to reveal this secret and also to give the potency via this lecture. When you read, listen or gain access to this Lecture Revelation in any other form, then all will be well with you, from the spirit, to the soul, to the physical truth.

Secondly, who is man that makes **ME**, **THE FATHER GOD THE CREATOR OF THE UNIVERSE** to be so serious about bringing **MY WORD** back on earth for the edification of man? What does man stand for? Why do **I** attribute so much **IMPORTANCE** to man? Why should **GOD** of heaven and earth, **HE IS THE SPIRIT, THE SUPREME BEING** that has no problem in any form bother so much about man?

Today, **I** shall give you some insight into this. It is because physically, **I** do not have any other dwelling place apart from mankind. Man is **THE FATHER GOD'S** estate. **HE IS THE SPIRIT** lives in every living creature and living organism, but those cannot give **ME** any **GLORY** in a meaningful way apart from mankind.

When you hear that **GOD** created this and that in seven days then rested, it was actually many generations past and thousands and millions of years for each of the creations to develop and to improve to have **WISDOM**, to **UNDERSTAND** who **THE FATHER GOD** is, and to **WORSHIP THE FATHER GOD** in **SPIRIT** and in **TRUTH**, but they do not. For this reason, they could not give **ME** the **DIVINED** fruit that **I** should gain from all **MY** creation in general. As a result, **I** called **MYSELF** into **MYSELF** and all **MYSELF** and assembled all **MY POSITIVE SELVES** as **G.O.D** and **G.O.C** at a meeting where **I** said, '*LET* us create man in **OUR IMAGE** and **MY OWN LIKENESS**'. Had **I** said that we should create man in the **IMAGE** only, then man would be the **PHYSICAL GLORY** alone which is for the mother **GOD** as what you see is what you take. However, **I AM THE SPIRIT** and also the **PHYSICAL TRUTH**, therefore **I** decided to attach the **LOVE** of **MYSELF** to man, which is **MY LIKENESS** as the **WISDOM** of **EVERYTHING**. And as humans, created, not only in the image but also in **MY** likeness then, they should behave like **I, THE FATHER GOD**, their **CREATOR**. Children that are good should behave as their good parents. This means that the offspring comes from the father and the mother, as the womb that helps the offspring to generate as the good parents.

Adam was the offspring of **THE FATHER GOD** on earth as the first mansion building of **THE FATHER GOD**. **I** lived in him and gave names to all the creations, because every **WORD** that came out from Adam was the **TRUTH** and that is why all the creations have their correct names. **I** was happy and **BLESSED** all the creations. Eventually, because of improvement and development, **I** attached the spirit of experimentation and training of **EVOLUTION** so that man would have opportunity to develop. Do not forget that **MY** actual **AIM** and **OBJECTIVE** was to gain **MY GLORY** in order that man would **KNOW THE FATHER GOD** and **UNDERSTAND** who **THE FATHER GOD** is, thereby **LOVING THE FATHER GOD** and themselves.

Show **ME** a human being that has been born into this world that has **LOVE** for another human being. Since human beings have taken **EVOLUTION** from other natures to be born into this world to live and interact with other natures such as birds, fishes, animals and other living creatures that have come as human beings, they have hated themselves. They fight, quarrel and kill each other, and have brought a rampant system on earth because of their low mentality as subhuman beings in nature. **MY AIM** is for human beings to have **LOVE** as **I THE FATHER GOD** is **LOVE** and there is the likeness of **GOD** in man as **LOVE** and **WISDOM**. Whoever that **UNDERSTANDS** and has **WISDOM** must surely **LOVE**. And must surely be **PEACEFUL** and must surely have **MERCY** and must surely be a **RIGHTEOUS** person, a perfect and complete human in nature of **THE FATHER GOD**. The reason why **I** created the physical world was to bring every creation that **I** had in spirit into the physical reality via the **SPOKEN WORD**. And this was for the purpose and process of education, so that, in this world, everyone would **KNOW ME, THE FATHER GOD THE CREATOR OF THE UNIVERSE** and give **ME, MY DUE GLORY** as their **CREATOR** and their **SUPREME FATHER GOD ALMIGHTY, THE UNIVERSAL SUPREME WORD**.

MY HOUSE, MY ESTATE, AND MY MANSION

I have been going through the educational processes with humans for many, many generations, but **I** was not attributed **MY** full **GLORY**, because no one cared about the existence of **THE FATHER**, their **CREATOR**. People pretend because they are the enemy of **GOOD** things and quart spirits as parasitic flashing pass-by in nature, the error, the second hand and undeveloped nature, which is Satan the father of all evil that has come into the world to destroy the house that **I** have built for **MYSELF**. For that reason **I, THE SPOKEN WORD** as revealed through this Lecture Revelation, and has decided to come back and renovate **MY HOUSE, MY ESTATE**, and **MY MANSION** which was Adam. After Adam, **I** came back as Our Lord Jesus Christ. Our Lord Jesus Christ was born among the Jews, but he was not an ordinary human being. He is that

THING that was born through **THE HOLY SPIRIT**. That **THING** means **THE WORD**, as **THE MAKER OF HEAVEN** and **EARTH**. Our **LORD JESUS CHRIST** was that **THING** as the **SPIRIT** of **CREATION** and **THE CREATOR HIMSELF**. **I THE SPIRIT OF TRUTH** was His **INNER SELF** because **I** was his complete system as **IMAGE** and **LIKENESS**, and the **LIKENESS** is **THE SPIRIT**, whilst the **IMAGE** is the physical **TRUTH**. **OUR LORD JESUS CHRIST** came in the **IMAGE** of Adam and the **LIKENESS** of **ME** as **THE SUPREME GOD, THE CREATOR OF THE UNIVERSE** because **THE HOLY SPIRIT** was **INSIDE** of Him and that is **THE SPOKEN WORD**. The **SPOKEN WORD** is the **LIKENESS** and the **WISDOM** whilst the **IMAGE** is your physical body. For that reason, **I** have now come today to give this Lecture Revelation to reveal who **I AM**, since **I** have given the insight of **MYSELF** as **THE SPOKEN WORD MANIFEST** from **REAL** to **REALSO**

and from **REALSO** to **AMISO** which means, from **SPIRIT** to **SOUL** and from **SOUL** to **PHYSICAL**.

INFINITY IN CAPACITY

I AM THE ALPHA and **OMEGA**, the **BEGINNING** and ever **FRONT BEGINNING**, without an end; **UNLIMITED** and **INDEFINITE** in **NATURE** and **INFINITY** in **CAPACITY**, as such, **I** have to give this Lecture Revelation today to enhance all **POSITIVE** human souls who know themselves to be human **GODS** and any other type of human being that is breathing **THE WORD**, because they can, voluntarily, take an **EVOLUTION** to know **THE FATHER** through **UNDERSTANDING** from **THE FATHER'S TALK (GOD PRESENT)**, and through the **HIGHER SELF SCHOOL OF BROTHERHOOD MASTERSHIP**. This will **IMPROVE** your nature so that you will be rejoicing and be **SHORT LISTED** and be **APPOINTED** and **RULE** with **GOD**

THE FATHER for eternity. That means that your **SOUL** has **CONTINUITY** with **THE FATHER GOD** which is what Christ meant by saying, '**MY FATHER** and **I** is **ONE**'.

KEY A: INTRODUCTION

The introduction of this Lecture Revelation is about **THE SPOKEN WORD** and **HOW TO SPEAK THE WORD**. In every situation, there is an **INSTRUCTION** and **DESCRIPTION**, which is the manual book of operation. Today, **I AM** giving the **MANUAL** of **THE WORD**. It has pleased **ME THE FATHER GOD ALMIGHTY** after many, many generations before today to bring this **MANUAL**. This is the beginning of **THE GLORY** of **GOD'S** generation as the final and spiritual digital age. The age of **THE GLORY** of **GOD** is to reveal this enhanced companion Lecture Revelation that would make every human soul happy because it would bring a short cut to help all souls. Today is the AO of AO of OG (the tenth of the tenth month of the year two thousand and seven). From OA to AO of **FATHER** OG is when **I** decided to reveal the **MANUAL** of **THE WORD**, the **INSTRUCTION BOOK**, and the **COMPANION BOOK** for the **ENHANCEMENT** for all **SPEAKERS**. Man stands for the **HOUSE** and the **SPEAKER** of **THE WORD**. Man is the **LOUDSPEAKER**, a **BOX**, created and kept physically as an **IMAGE** with an inbuilt **INTERNAL CONDUCTOR**, and **TRANSISTOR** that **GENERATES** inside as a spirit. This means that when **I SPEAK** in **MY STUDIO**, as **THE SUPREME THOUGHT** of **THE FATHER** then, the **GENERATING FORCE** would materialise the **SOUND** through you, a human person in the natural box of selves called a **HUMAN BEING**. And that is the **GEN** of all things which is the **AMPLIFIER** of the **SPOKEN WORD** that **I** have built inside man and that is a spirit that no scientist knows about. This **AMPLIFIER** is

THE FATHER GOD'S ENERGY as **THE SPIRITUAL WAVE** called **GEN** the **AMPLIFIER** of **THE WORD**. This **GEN** is acting as a **CONDUCTOR**, and also a **TRANSITING** energy component that when **I GENERATE** as **THE FATHER GOD**, it enables man as a living soul to **SPEAK**. Not every living creature or organism can **SPEAK**, but human beings can, and since human beings can **SPEAK THE WORD, I** have never, before now given anyone the **DIRECTIVE** or an **INSTRUCTION MANUAL** or **DESCRIPTIVE BOOK** or an **ENHANCEMENT** companion of the **SPOKEN WORD**. People know that **THE WORD** is **GOD**, but which **WORD** is **GOD**? People know that **THE WORD** is **ME THE FATHER GOD, THE SON**, and **THE HOLY SPIRIT**, but which type of **WORD** are they? How did they know what **THE WORD** is, yet every living human being can **SPEAK**? What are they **SPEAKING** about, and what type of **WORD** are they **SPEAKING**. They are rapping on about negative and evil words that create so many bad things on earth. If you read the Lecture Revelation titled; **THE PARTICLE OF CREATION**, you will understand how the evil things are not created by **ME THE FATHER GOD** rather they are created by the **SMALL BOX** which **I THE FATHER GOD** created for **MYSELF**, as the old masters with their **SPRINTER** of **TONGUES**. However that is not the focus of today's Lecture Revelation.

Today's Lecture Revelation is to provide all human beings with the **MANUAL BOOK OF THE SPOKEN WORD**, the **INSTRUCTION** book and **ENHANCEMENT** of how to **SPEAK** so that from the day you have access to this Lecture Revelation, you will know that if you **SPEAK** outside of this **INSTRUCTION**, then you will be seriously queried by **ME THE SUPREME WORD OF THE UNIVERSE**.

THE CREATOR OF HEAVEN AND EARTH

In the **BEGINNING** was **THE WORD** and **THE WORD** was with **GOD** and that **WORD** is **GOD, THE CREATOR OF HEAVEN AND EARTH**. Therefore, every human being that is born into this world starts to **SPEAK** either before or after eighteen months. After twelve months, the child would start to **SPEAK** a meaningful **WORD** and by eighteen months, the quality of their **SPEAKING** would have improved until they start to **SPEAK** well, but where is the **MANUAL** of directive of how to speak? From today henceforth, the father or the mother must present everyone that is born into this world, with this **MANUAL**. Every human being including kings, queens, presidents, prime ministers, head of states, army men, preachers, teachers and indeed any field of endeavour provided that they **SPEAK** must have a copy of this **MANUAL** as a compulsory requirement.

This is the **MANUAL** of **HOW TO SPEAK**. This **MANUAL** is **THE WORD** which **I** have given through this Lecture Revelation to help you to become a **POSITIVE** part of the creation of **GOD** so that you would not destroy your soul.

This introductory part of the Lecture Revelation is about **HOW TO THINK** and **HOW TO SPEAK** so as to **MANIFEST** a **GOOD** event. **I AM** going to explain why people cannot **SPEAK WELL**. People do not **SPEAK WELL** because they do not **THINK WELL**. However, **I** have made it clear that this Lecture Revelation is compulsory for every human being that **SPEAKS**. If you can talk, or cork or **SPEAK** or indeed any how that you do with **THE WORD**, either you are putting it into writing, or looking at it in the eye, or talking via your hands (signing), and any other way that you may do, in so far as you know the meaning of **THE WORD** and you can manipulate it by **THOUGHT**, or

SPEECH, then you must have this **MANUAL OF THE SPOKEN WORD**, on **HOW SPEAK THE WORD**. A copy should be given and made assessable to every human being. When a child is born, their caretaker should read this to them before they are a year in age. Also, their parents or their care taker should give a copy to them. If they do not adhere to the **INSTRUCTIONS**, their blood would be upon them and they cannot blame anyone. Every **IMAGE** that does not **SPEAK** well according to the **INSTRUCTION** of this **MANUAL** cannot be **MY LIVING HOUSE** of **THE FATHER GOD**. They would be discarded as a nuisance and something that is not **GOOD** and **I** will put them off. There is no need to build a complex of houses when you will not live there. From the moment that you decide that you will not be living there, you should destroy the complex and build another one and that is why when some people die, their soul is destroyed forever because they do not **SPEAK WELL**. If you do not want to be destroyed forever then make sure that you take today's Lecture Revelation as a very important one.

KEY B: **THE WORD OF PEACE**

If you **THINK WELL** and have the mind of **GOD** and want a progressive future then you should join the **SCHOOL OF THE HIGHER SELF BROTHERHOOD MASTERSHIP** or visit **GOD'S** spiritual Library, called the **ENCYCLOPAEDIA OF INFINITY** of **GOD**, "**KING SOLOMON SPIRITUAL LIBRARY**". If you visit the library and follow all the Lecture Revelations in a step by step fashion then you will have the **UNDERSTANDING** to become a **POSITIVE MASTER**. If you **FOCUS** on **THE MASTER SELF** then you will develop and have **UNDERSTANDING** and **KNOWLEDGE** about everything that **I** have thought. With this, you will now know that you have to **THINK WELL** all the time and develop a **TRUTHFUL SPIRIT** which means that you must be **TRUTHFUL** to yourself which is your **THOUGHT**. When you **THINK WELL** it means that you are a **WELL** person. When you **SPEAK** exactly what you **THINK** then you would create an event for the edification of everybody and that is why if you **THINK** differently from what you **SPEAK** then you are evil and you will surely have problems with **THE FATHER**, your **CREATOR**. However, you have the opportunity to **THINK** first and if the **THOUGHT** that comes to you is negative and from your lower mind, that is your negative self, then, you should not approve of that **THOUGHT**. First, send your idea from your mind back to the reason faculty of your brain. The **REASON** faculty would discuss with your **THINKING** faculty and between the two, they will suggest which **WORD** that should come out. The suggestion would be sent back to the heart, the home base of **THE HOLY SPIRIT**, which is **ME THE FATHER GOD** living in you and that is where the decision is taken in your heart after due consultation, then the hyphen would release **THE WORD**. At this point when you **SPEAK**, you will be **SPEAKING** a well organized and arranged **WORD** that would help others like this Lecture Revelation of this day.

The Lecture Revelation that you are hearing or reading is a generating energy from the **SUPREME STUDIO** of **THE FATHER GOD**. The actual **STUDIO** of **MYSELF** is **MY** real **SELF** and that is why **I AM POSSESSING** HRM King Solomon David Jesse **ETE** in whom, **I** have built "**MY DIVINE SUPREME SPIRITUAL POSITIVE TRANSFORMER AND TRANSMITTER GENERATING TRANSISTOR SUPER WAVE OF THE HOLY SPIRIT OF TRUTH SELF MASTERSHIP**" from the beginning of time so that every time that **I** want to **TALK MY WORDS**, it would come out **WELL ARRANGED**. And that is the

UNLIMITED CAPACITY MEMORY INTERMODOM MODIOBOM that **I** have given to HRM King Solomon David Jesse **ETE**. With this **BOM**, **I** can bring out every **POSITIVE SELF** and every **POSITIVE** idea that **I, THE FATHER GOD** has buried in the **ARCHIVE RECORD** without any ceremony. However, **I** first had to squeeze him and train him spiritually on how to have **SELF AWARENESS** and to know that he is not supposed to **SPEAK** any negative **WORD**, rather he should **THINK WELL**. And he has passed a certain level, although he is not perfect, but has done more than any other person has yet done, because of **MY HOLY SPIRIT OF CHRIST OF THE FATHER GOD** in him. As a result, he has been elevated and **I** have chosen him again to be **TALKING** through and that is why **THE FATHER'S TALK (GOD PRESENT)** is wonderful. For this reason, the elevated mind which is the **SELF AWARENESS** as the **HIGHERSELF** has led him to **THINK**

WELL all the time. He has no time for thinking evil about anyone. He does not get jealous or is he involved in other negativisms, never! HRM King Solomon **ETE** is always focusing on **ME THE FATHER GOD**, **THE FATHER GOD, THE FATHER GOD, GOOD, GOOD, GOOD** and **PEACE, PEACE, PEACE**. Left to him alone, the whole world would have experienced capital **JOY** and **PEACE**. For this reason, **I** have decided to use him, via his mouth, as the echo of **DIVINE ORDER** to release most of the **WISDOM** that **I** have had in store for many, many generations now. This Lecture Revelation does not come from the mind that is stupid or the mind that turns up and down. It comes from the steady mind and the **TRUTHFUL** heart with the power of *"COMPREHENSIVE AND ABILITY INSTINCT OF SUPREME MEMORY"* **THE DIVINE INSTINCT OF GOD'S WISDOM.**

I THE FATHER GOD has **DIVINED** the heart of the Senior Christ Servant King Solomon David Jesse **ETE** for **MYSELF** and that is why **I POSSESS** him and live inside him so that when **I TALK**, he, as the **SPEAKER**, with an **INBUILT MEMORY** called **COMPREHENSIVE** and **ABILITY MEMORY** would echo the **WORD** out. If he commits any error, **I** forgive him because **I AM IN CHARGE** in him. And **I** want to do this for everyone who is a true servant of **GOD**.

Take **EVOLUTION** by **ACCEPTING** this **WORD** and **THINK WELL**, and you would bring forth **THE WORD** of **PEACE** because **THE WORD** of **PEACE** can only come from a **PEACEFUL** heart. If you are annoyed for one second, you cannot **SPEAK** a **GOOD WORD**. If you are confused for just a second, you cannot **SPEAK** a **GOOD WORD**. If you **THINK WELL** you will be **PEACEFUL** and that is when you will know that you are a servant of **GOD**. **ALWAYS SPEAK**

THE WORD OF PEACE as the **WORD** that makes every hearer to benefit. There are always two **THOUGHTS** and two **MINDS** that arise, but you must use **MY SECOND THOUGHT** the careful mind which **I** used to manifest King Solomon David physically on earth the first time as incarnated ABEL the positive second son of the universal Father ADAM, therefore you must also use it to manifest **POSITIVE** pronouncement. When a thought arises in your heart, telling you that you should kill, you should go to war, you should destroy, you should say this and say that, generating all kinds of evil and negativism, you must rebuke that thought by saying **GOD FORBID BAD THING**. By so doing, you will give a chance for the **SECOND THOUGHT** to consider whether you should carry out that thought or not and that is when you start to have **THE HIGHER SELF**. Anyone who listens or reads this Lecture Revelation and adheres to the teaching would be **WELL** in all capacities of life. This is not a matter of a secret society, when the old masters hid many things and used it to make money. This is the **LOVE** of **THE FATHER GOD**, the **SCHOOL** of **THE HIGHER SELF BROTHERHOOD MASTERSHIP** which is open to every soul. The **WORD** of **PEACE** which is the **PEACE** of **THE FATHER** is 'Solomon Etteh' because Solomon in Hebrew means **PEACE** as Shalom-Sharon, and **ETE** means **FATHER** in Efik or Ibibio, therefore the combination of the two names stands for **PEACE** of **THE FATHER** as Shalom of **GOD** as Solomon Abba, Solomon **ETE**, and Abba – **FATHER**. As result, the **WORD** of **PEACE** came from the **COMPREHENSIVE MIND** as the mind that generates a **PEACEFUL** co-existence in **UNDERSTANDING** and **SUPREME WISDOM**.

KEY C: **THE WORD OF LOVE**

If you **SPEAK THE WORD** of **PEACE** then you will always have a calm spirit which makes for a calm nerve, and then **LOVE** will manifest through **PEACE**. You cannot **LOVE** someone if you and the person are not in perfect good mind of **PEACE**. You cannot **LOVE** someone that you do not think well of. If you think **PEACEFULLY** and behave **PEACEFULLY** as the **SECOND THOUGHT** about everyone in a calm manner, then the **WORD** of **LOVE** can materialise. The **WORD** of **LOVE** is very important for the **POSITIVE** creation. Any time that you **SPEAK** the **WORD** of **LOVE** from the **PEACEFUL** heart then what will come out from you will be **LOVE**, **GOOD CREATION**, and a **GOOD** atmosphere. People know of the **SPOKEN WORD**, but they do not know about the **THOUGHT**; however the **WORD** comes from the **THOUGHT** which is the home of **THE FATHER GOD** as **THE FATHER'S SPIRIT** called **SILENT THOUGHT**. The twin self of **THE FATHER'S POTENCY** is what **I** used in creation which was **THE DESIGNER**, as **THE**

THOUGHT and **THE MAKER** as **THE WORD**. The **DESIGNER** and the **SPOKEN WORD** is the **TWIN SELF** called **WISDOM** and the **MAKER** as the **REASON** and the **WORD**, the **THOUGHT** and the **WORD**, and it is this, **MY TWIN SELF** that manifests **MY GLORY**.

I came before as **CHRIST** the **SPOKEN WORD** to bring everyone into **ORDER**, and now **I** have manifested as **THE FATHER'S TALK** and as the **WISDOM** so that every **DESIGN** would be **WELL** created which will and manifest **WELL** and would be **WELL** managed and **WELL** arranged. The **WORD** of **LOVE** comes from the **PEACEFUL** heart and the **WORD** of **LOVE** means a **PEACEFUL** co-existence. **LOVE** is **GOD, PEACE** is **GOD,** and anything **GOOD** is **GOD**. From **PEACE, LOVE** manifests therefore if you do not have **PEACE** you cannot **LOVE** as such the **WORD** of **PEACE** is part of the **INSTRUCTION** to adhere to, in that when you want to **SPEAK** you must consult with **PEACE** in your heart, then you will make a **GOOD** pronouncement with the **WORD** of **LOVE**. Remember that **LOVE** is not fornication or intercourse. **LOVE** means **MY POSITIVE SELF** of **THE FATHER GOD LOVE**, **LOVE**, and **LOVE**. Through **LOVE**, you conquer all evil and through **LOVE**, everything becomes **WELL**. Those who practise **LOVE** and **SPEAK** the **WORD** of **PEACE** cannot go to war, they cannot hate, they cannot kill, and they cannot do any evil because the **WORD** of **LOVE** is **GOD**.

KEY D: **THE WORD OF MERCY**

Through the **WORD** of **LOVE**, **MERCY** manifests itself. Anytime that you are **SPEAKING** the **WORD** of **LOVE** you will automatically show **MERCY** because **MERCY** is the proof that **GOD** is around and the atmosphere is **GOOD** and the area is welcoming. To show **MERCY** without judgement is what is expected. **MERCY** and **LOVE, RIGHTEOUSNESS, KINDNESS** and **PEACE** signify the kingdom of **THE FATHER GOD, THE HOLY SPIRIT** and that is the **HOUSE** where the **HOST** of **GOD** dwells. If you **THINK WELL** and **SPEAK WELL**, the **WORD** of **MERCY** would always come from your mouth. It should be the **WORD** that when you **SPEAK** everyone becomes happy, the **WORD** that when you **SPEAK** it becomes a **BLESSING**, and the **WORD** that when you **SPEAK** it would reconstruct a bad situation and the **WORD** that when you **SPEAK, THE FATHER GOD'S POTENCY** would generate itself and stamp it for you as a **MERCIFUL WORD. THE WORD** that when **SPEAK**, it does not condemn people and **THE WORD** that when people fight, you will know how to **SPEAK** and bring **PEACE** among them and **THE WORD** that can make every country to unite and make **PEACE**. A **PEACEFUL WORD**, a

WORD of **LOVE**, and a **WORD** of **MERCY** can never bring wars, can never bring confusion, can never create knock-a-head's and can never bring problems of any kind, but when you **SPEAK** outside of this as an evil politician, then you bring problems into the world.

This Lecture Revelation is called **THE ADMINISTRATOR**, as the key and **ENHANCEMENT** of the **GENERAL DIRECTIVES** and **MANUAL** to be used in governing the whole world.

KEY E: **THE RIGHTEOUS WORD**

The **RIGHTEOUS WORD** manifests because you **SPEAK MERCIFULLY**. You should show **MERCY** when you make a pronouncement because you know that every **WORD** would come to pass as creation. If you say things like, 'we would not go to that war and we will find another way to resolve our differences, so that we would live in **PEACE**' then you are a

RIGHTEOUS person. Also **WORDS** such as 'we would not retaliate for what that person has done rather, we would find another way to bring that man into order would make you a **RIGHTEOUS** person. Why does a president not **SPEAK** in this manner, and why does an army man not **SPEAK** such **WORDS** instead of warring and killing and causing untold havoc for people, when there are other methods that man can employ for world peace? There are remedies which do not involve war and there are **WORDS** of **RIGHTEOUSNESS**. If you **SPEAK WELL**, it would barrier wars. If you **SPEAK** the **WORD** of **MERCY, LOVE**, and **PEACE**, then you are automatically a **RIGHTEOUS** man, a man that **GOD** dwells in and that means **I** can make you the servant of **GOD** to lead the entire world and take care of all the creation of **GOD**. If you **THINK WELL** and **SPEAK WELL** because you have a **PEACEFUL** heart then that brings out **MERCIFUL WORDS** that would automatically manifest the **WORD** of **RIGHTEOUSNESS**.

A **RIGHTEOUS WORD** is the **WORD** that barriers wars and problems. Not **WORDS** such as; 'leave that man he is too troublesome'. Not **WORDS** such as; 'if that were me I would not marry him because he a very bad man'. And 'leave that woman she is a prostitute' and all those type of words that people **SPEAK** are not **RIGHTEOUS WORDS** because you speak them to cause problems, but if you **THINK WELL** and **SPEAK WELL** then your **WORD** becomes a **RIGHTEOUS WORD** and then **THE HOLY SPIRIT** would direct you.

KEY F: **THE WORD OF KINDNESS**

You will now realise that **THE RIGHTEOUS WORD** will manifest **THE WORD** of **KINDNESS**. You should say **WORDS** such as; 'give this man that thing or do not imprison him, forgive him, leave him to go, discharge and acquit him. I will pay his dept or come and I will give you something to eat or come and see me and I will help you to establish in business. And come to my house if you have no where to live and I will give you my boys-quarters to live or I will pay your rent for you'. These are the **WORDS** of **KINDNESS**. The **WORD** of **KINDNESS** emerges when you **FORGIVE** people and forget, then that is **RIGHTEOUSNESS**. A **RIGHTEOUS WAY** is to find a way that is better than the other way and that is the **UPPER** and **POSITIVE** way that you should use to deal with every situation which is better than the lower and negative way, and when you **SPEAK** that **WORD** it would create a **GOOD** situation and a nice environment. Since the **RIGHTEOUS WORD** has created a **GOOD** situation, the **WORD** of **KINDNESS** would follow with such **WORDS** as 'do not worry I give you back what you have lost. I will build that place for you, lets continue to live together, I **FORGIVE** you and will not count that sin for you and do not do that thing again, I am sorry, had I known I would not have said that'. These are the **KIND WORDS** as **THE WORD** of **CHARITY**, the **WORD** of **LOVE**, the **WORD** of **PEACE** and that is **HOW** you should **SPEAK**. If you continue to **SPEAK KIND WORDS** that gives **HOPE** to people in every situation then that makes you a child of **GOD**.

When someone is sick, you should say 'do not worry because that sickness would not kill you'. When someone is in lack, you should say 'do not worry let me see what I can do to help you', and other **WORDS** such as, 'you will win this contest, you will have this job', and these are **POSITIVE** and **KIND WORDS**. Even if you do not donate anything physically, but the **WORD** of **KINDNESS** that you have **SPOKEN** to that person has made the person to receive their wish. Always promise people with **KINDNESS** and encourage people to **SPEAK POSITIVE WORDS**. Use **WORDS** such as 'you will not die, you will not be sick, **FATHER GOD ALMIGHTY** has taken control, and everything is well for you'. These are all **KIND WORDS** and do not **SPEAK** negative **WORDS** outside of that. **SPEAK POSITIVELY** all the time which would manifest **KIND WORDS**. It does not require money or any other thing only to make a pronouncement about a situation when someone is in need and has a problem, and if you can follow that with a gesture then that is also **GOOD**. Make **POSITIVE** pronouncements as the **WORD** of **KINDNESS**. All children of God, all preachers, all the **SENIOR CHRIST SERVANTS** and all the kings and queens and all the prime ministers, all the heads of states, all the presidents, the fathers, the mothers, the senior brothers, sisters and all others in various positions, such as managers or directors, must **SPEAK** the **WORDS**. Show **KINDNESS** to people and do not make them to be frustrated, because of their problems, rather use **KIND WORDS** to give them **PEACE** and to soothe them. Even if you do not have anything in terms of material gain to offer, do you also not have a **WORD** of **KINDNESS to SPEAK**. And with that **I THE FATHER GOD** would **USE** those **WORDS** to materialise something **GOOD** for the person, because **THE WORD CREATES EVENTS**, In the Name and the Blood of Our Lord Jesus Christ, *Amien*.

ENYE ODUDU ABASI MI OOO ZIM ZIM ZIM ASSASSU, POSITIVE, POSITIVE, POSITIVE!

KEY G: **THE WORD OF TRUTH**

As you can see the **WORD** of **PEACE**, the **WORD** of **LOVE**, the **RIGHTEOUS WORD, the MERCIFUL WORD** and the **WORD** of **KINDNESS** generates in you according to how you think. The song that sings as:

MERCY and **LOVE**, **RIGHTEOUSNESS, KINDNESS** and **PEACE** signify **THE TRUTH**. **THE TRUTH** means the Kingdom of **GOD** as **I THE SUPREME FATHER GOD** is **THE TRUTH. THE SPIRIT OF TRUTH** has manifested in the world as **OOO**. People ask what is the meaning of **LEADER OLUMBA OLUMBA OBU**? And **I** ask why do you argue about the name? **OOO** stands for **OMNIPOTENT, OMNIPRESENT** and **OMNISCIENT** which means **OMINILOVE, OMINIMERCY, OMINIPEACE, OMINIRIGHTEOUSNESS, OMINIKINDNESS**, and **OMINITRUTH. I AM THE MANIFESTATION PERSONIFIED HOLY SPIRIT OF TRUTH** from Adam to Christ to **OLUMBA. I** do not pretend. **I** as **LEADER OLUMBA OLUMBA OBU** came to dwell in the **HOUSE**, the **SUPREME BUILDING** on earth called the **MANSION HALL**. **I** was born in a small town called **BIAKPAN**, which is **THE NEW**

JERUSALEM. Do you hear **MY** voice anywhere? Do **I** make noise; rather **I** stay behind to control the front. **I** stay behind to manipulate things spiritually because **I AM** not a showing off **SPIRIT**. And besides if **I AM THE HOLY SPIRIT OF TRUTH PERSONIFIED**, then everything and everywhere is **ME THE FATHER GOD** therefore why should **I** make noise in a small corner. Who is America, who is Britain, who is Africa? It is **ME THE FATHER GOD** and every creation is **THE FATHER GOD**, but if you turn that creation to be negative, then you will pay for it, because all negativism would wax away. You will see that from now onwards, **I** will gradually eradicate all negativisms and **POSITIVISM** would take its place and stand for eternity in the Name and Blood of Our Lord Jesus Christ, *Amien*. This **WORD** of **TRUTH** that is manifesting represents **ME, THE HOLY SPIRIT of TRUTH, FATHER OLUMBA OLUMBA OBU** as **THE KING OF KINGS** and **THE LORD OF**

LORDS, THE SPOKEN WORD on, *HOW* to *USE ME*. Do not say that **THE FATHER** says this and **THE FATHER** says that and therefore you go about involving and doing negative things. If you use the **WORD** for any negativism, you are not using **ME**, and **I** will disgrace you. If you use **THE FATHER GOD** in the **POSITIVE** way by **SPEAKING** the **WORD** of **PEACE**, the **WORD** of **LOVE**, the **WORD** of **MERCY**, the **WORD** of **RIGHTEOUSNESS** and the **WORD** of **KINDNESS** then **THE SPIRIT** of **TRUTH** as **THE WORD OF TRUTH** will automatically materialise. Then **I THE FATHER GOD** would **TALK** through you, because the **TRUTHFUL** heart is where **THE SPIRIT OF TRUTH** resides, therefore **I** will stand with you both in the spirit and in the physical truth. Someone who does not **THINK** any negative about anybody, someone who does not gossip about anyone and does not have any evil mind for anyone rather, he or she **THINKS** only about **THE FATHER**

GOD'S GLORY and how things should be **GOOD** in the whole world. Someone who has the mind for the generality of **EQUALITY** of life for everyone and that is what **I** have come to establish in this world. **I** will direct and **TALK** through any government official; any king, any individual, any man, any woman or child that has such a mind. From the day that you read or hear this **FATHER'S TALK** or read this Lecture Revelation, "**THE MANUAL AND DIRECTIVE OF HOW TO SPEAK THE WORD**" and you stop thinking evil, stop planning evil and having bad wishes for people, and thinking nonsense about your-self, then your are blessed.

Read the Lecture Revelation titled, **DIVINE ATTENTION** then you will see that all bad spirits and formulated evil spirits come from a formulated evil mind. When you are narrow in **UNDERSTANDING** and without **WISDOM** then that is the problem.

Refer to the Lecture Revelation titled, **BABY SPIRIT**. Read all **THE FATHER'S** Lecture Revelations or at least seven titles and you would be elevated and when **I** say elevated, **I** mean really elevated, because every of **THE FATHER'S TALK** comes with a **POTENCY** that can automatically change you. **AS I AM TALKING NOW** if you **BELIEVE** this **WORD** and take this training and teaching and put, it into practice, then you will become a newly arranged person with an arranged mind and arranged soul and with a new environment. Even if it happens that **I THE FATHER GOD** transfers you through death, **I** will send you back as a servant of **GOD** or **I** can decide to keep you here as long as **I** can use you to change the environment and to do what is **GOOD**.

You must always **SPEAK THE TRUTH** because **THE TRUE WORD** sets everybody free and do not deviate from **THE TRUTH**, and from **MY** teaching because **I** have come as **THE SUPERNATURAL TEACHER** and **I AM** passing through King Solomon **ETE** via **THE FATHER'S TALK** (**GOD PRESENT**) to bring the **TESTIMONY** of **EVERLASTING GOSPEL**. The **ORIGINAL PLAIN TRUTH** has been set on earth. **I SPEAK THE TRUTH** and **MANIFEST THE TRUTH**. In the Kingdom of **GOD**, **I** do not want second hand practices and second hand ideas. Before now **I** have set everything in order and given a comprehensive handbook for the doctrine of the new kingdom, and no one should add or subtract to that. Everything should go back to the way that **I** had kept it in the kingdom of **GOD**, the New Jerusalem which is **MY** wife. The kingdom of **GOD** is **MY** wife which **I** prepared from heaven and brought down here to establish therefore, **I** do not want anybody to buy anything for **MY** wife. Do not buy under-wear for **MY** wife and do not buy even brassier for **MY** wife. Are you spirited enough to bring the slightest idea in the system, which is the kingdom of **GOD**? Are you in spirit, then where are you? Have you passed from *ABC quasi, quasi, quack*, (a babyish understanding). Do you even know who you are, and if you do not know who you are, how then do you begin to contribute to **GOD'S** business? **I** have established everything in Brotherhood of the Cross and Star as the kingdom of **GOD** on earth and not a church before now, and **I** have kept quite, because Brotherhood is not a church, and it is not pertaining to a particular country. It is universal in phenomenon, and lavishly covers all creation seen and unseen, heard and unheard, touchable and untouchable. That is the meaning of Brotherhood and that includes Lucifer herself. However, **I** have separated everything **GOOD** as the **POSITIVE** part, from the negative part of Brotherhood. **I** have formed the **DIVINE** part of Brotherhood with **THE HOLY SPIRIT** as **MY DIVINE SELF** by doing away with the other **SELF**. Do you not defecate away any bad thing in your system? When you eat nice food and drink water, after twenty hours you will defecate the bad part of the food away and only the **GOOD** part of the food will remain in you, therefore **I** have defecated all the nonsense and the entire negative, and all ideas that **I** used as experimentation when **I** was doing creation completely away. Lower people **SPEAK** without due care thereby, creating all sorts of evils. **I** have done away with all that as everybody does to faeces. If you decide to utilise those ideas in the name of your father and mother's traditions which are formed by women, men and small, small children, with natural baby and negative spirits in them or a person who is the offspring of a negative doctor and a soothsayer then that has nothing to do with **ME THE FATHER GOD**. And if you decide to use ideas from dragon spit girls who go about fornicating and doing all sorts of things, then again it has nothing to do with **ME**. When such people give ideas and suggestions that Brotherhood should be this and that, what sort off audacity are they trying to portray? In the whole world no one should make any contribution towards the **WORD**, because **THE WORD** is the **ADMINISTRATOR**, but if you have an **ENLIGHTENED MIND** and **WISDOM** as King Solomon then **I** will give you the power to **RE-ARRANGE** other human beings and then you become an **IMPUTE CENTRE**. King Solomon is now an **IMPUTE CENTRE** whom **I** use as a **COMPREHENSIVE MEMORY** to **ENLIGHTEN** mankind and if you attach yourself to that then you will surely take an **EVOLUTION** to a **HIGHER SELF** and all will be well with your soul in the name of Our Lord Jesus Christ.

CONCLUSION ONE: THE WORD OF WISDOM

This Lecture Revelation does not actually have a conclusion. It has no beginning and no end, because it is round, round and round. It is round there, round here and round everywhere, and that is the **SPOKEN WORD**. However **I** will stop this part of this Lecture Revelation at this conclusion stage.

THE WORD OF WISDOM

THE WORD of **WISDOM** is when you are in **TRUE** partnership with **ME THE FATHER GOD**, then all your **SPEECH** is **THE WORD** of **WISDOM**. If you read the Lecture Revelation titled **MASTERSHIP**, you will find that **WISDOM** is the chairman whilst **UNDERSTANDING** is the secretary. **UNDERSTANDING** is also the secretary to **KNOWLEDGE** therefore **WISDOM** and **KNOWLEDGE** work together. One is spiritual whilst the other is physical. The scientist used the **WISDOM** of Solomon in the physical way and manipulated it to have technology. Just as people have manufactured artificial flowers through copying the natural ones to the extent that when you see the artificial version of a lily or a sunflower, you would think them to be real. They have used the **KNOWLEDGE** gained from **WISDOM** and applied it to achieve useful products therefore; **WISDOM** and **KNOWLEDGE** are useful together when they are used **POSITIVELY**.

MONEY is **KNOWLEDGE** whilst **LOVE** is the **WISDOM**. **LOVE** and **MONEY** are the same just as a human being and **MONEY** are the same. The **LOVE** of **THE FATHER GOD** generates through the spirit of **GOODNESS** and **KINDNESS** to everyone around you such as your children, your mother, father, your friends, and others. You are to help them if and when you have the **MONEY** and that is the

KNOWLEDGE. The government is supposed to use **MONEY** to make everyone happy, not for going to war.

They are to make sure that every human being has enough **MONEY** in their pocket so that they can behave well. Also, they are to practise **LOVE**, because if everyone practices **LOVE** there would be no complain, because **LOVE** does everything well. **MONEY** is **KNOWLEDGE** in the place of **LOVE** which is **SPIRITUAL** and these two things can make the whole world to live very **PEACEFULLY** and **HAPPILY**. You should use the **LOVE** of **THE FATHER GOD** in using **MONEY** to minister through **WISDOM** and **UNDERSTANDING** as the secretary that helps everything to be well circulated. At present, **MONEY** is not being well circulated because **LOVE** is not being well circulated. If **EQUALITY** is in place through **WISDOM** then **MONEY** would circulate well. If you have **WISDOM** you would provide free electricity as a national gift to all mankind. If you have **WISDOM** you will provide free water, because water is free from **ME THE FATHER GOD**. If you have **WISDOM** you will provide free habitation so that everyone in the home such as the father, the mother, and every child or individual in the home would all have one room each. The national purse can do this, but in today's government, they do not do these things, because they do not have **LOVE** neither do they have **WISDOM**. Great Britain charges heavily for water by creating companies through privatisation for water which falls freely through the rain? How did they manufacture water, so that they should decide to charge so much for it?

Any king or president or prime minister who cannot put their feet down to have **LOVE** and **UNDERSTANDING**, so that they would share simple amenities such as water, electricity, gas, telephone and housing freely to all, which comes freely from **THE FATHER** cannot continue to rule. Since most of these amenities come free from **THE FATHER GOD**, you should transfer them from one country to another and engineer it so that everyone in the world gets access to these resources through **LOVE**, **WISDOM**, and **UNDERSTANDING** and you charge one simple tax to cover the cost and not for profit. It is only **MY** Divine spirit of **LOVE** through the **POWER** of **WISDOM** that can handle this. Do you not know that there is much money in the world to the extent that they do not know what to do with it? A few people in this world who collect it through their private companies contain it, and also the so called governments who are supposed to represent **ME THE FATHER GOD ALMIGHTY** waste all the money in evil programs by going to war and in other forms of negative practices.

The Spiritual General Manual Of Life

How can they charge for water, for communication systems and other such basic amenities? Do you ask how many millions that people make by buying shares? Why should people buy shares and make a lot of money whilst other people are suffering. Who keeps all this money and what do you do with all that money? This is the height of stupidity and idiocy, because if you have **WISDOM**, **UNDERSTANDING** and **LOVE** as a human being, and if you are not an animal, a coward and stupid, you cannot bank a lot of money in the bank, when there are poor people everywhere who do not have enough to eat, and where to live. And on top of that, you go about harassing them for council tax, water tax, and taxing everything, so that you will gain more whilst they are suffering. You do not have the sense to make everybody happy by ensuring that people have the very basics in life. You complain about arm robbers, you complain about thieves and fraudsters and all other dubious behaviours, but it is you who has caused some of those things to exist. Everybody is a human being as you are who has taste for good food, for good housing, for a car and every other thing that makes life enjoyable. However, those who do not have these things are seeing that you do not do much, but you live in a mansion, have untold number of cars and every other good thing as such what do you expect them to do? In fact, the government and all the so called big people that call themselves business tycoons and others that are singularly rich have contributed to the arm robbing, the prostitution, stealing, the criminal activity and evil practice by not equally distributing all amenities to everybody. You will come back and be a beggar, because if you are in the position to help others, but you do not, then when you die and come back, **I** will replace you with that person. Test **ME** and see! However there is a remedy to your problem.

King Solomon says vanity of vanities and became the prodigal son. Did you not hear the story that Our Lord Jesus the Christ gave about the prodigal son? **I AM** revealing today that story is about King Solomon. King Solomon is Abel incarnate and he was, and is a king. **I** brought him to be a king in the throne of his father David to rule Israel and he has tried a great deal, because since the reign of King Solomon, no one has made the efforts that he made, **I** mean not a single ruler has achieved what he did in terms of using **WISDOM** to make things well in recognition of **MY STATUS**. However he started taxing people, harassing them to make him rich. He ate well, married so many wives, and did all sorts of things ignoring the **LOVE** of **GOD** towards the general wellbeing of individual people, because he wanted to make his government stand well. As a result of his actions, **I** then made him King James in Great Britain to establish united front of universal charity, but people had a meeting and persuaded him to change charity to tax. Before this, there was nothing like politics, it was the rulership of the monarchy through the church (the system of **GOD'S** natural rulership) but after this, they formed, another wing called politics and formulated evil laws and all sort of things, and because of that, **I** relocated away from them. This time **I** put him in the village, and he is now complaining. This **FATHER'S TALK** that he is a witness to in terms of **SPEAKING** is via the village in Ikot Okwo –Nigeria Africa.

I was Abel's **FATHER ADAM** THE FIRST HUMAN GOD ON EARTH, and **I** was also **JESUS THE CHRIST**, and that is why **I** have revealed this today, because **I TALK** as **I** know. He was the prodigal son who took his entire share of wealth from his **FATHER**, and went and squandered it with women and all sorts of things and when he run out, he came and said that **I** should take him as a servant not as a son. **I** said OK, so it is his **WORD** that **I AM** using and that is why today 'Solomon' is a King servant. He is a servant of **GOD**, but he is HIS ROYAL MAJESTY KING SOLOMON, and people do not believe it, but it remains true, however through his servitude, **I AM** regaining his temple for him, because **I** do not live in the house that he built with his hand rather, **I** live inside him. It is through him that **I** can reveal all this things as Lectures Revelations to help humankind, because he is well enriched with **MY INNERSELF WISDOM**. As 'Solomon' is one with **ME**, **I** have kept him in this position, but if he was not **ME**, it is only **ME** who knows where **I** would have kept him. Would you really condemn your child when he misbehaves, when he is your blood, and particularly if that child comes back to apologise and sobers? Would you not have a kingdom for that child?

Today people talk about a kingdom out of a kingdom, but that is not so, it is the womb of **GOD**. There is a reason for everything, but **I AM** not going to go into that today, however, **I AM** revealing that King Solomon is the prodigal son, who said all is 'vanity of vanity'. And that is why today King Solomon has established **OLUMBA UNIVERSAL EQUALITY** and **OLUMBA UNIVERSAL THIS** and **THAT** where there will be free housing, free telephone, free water, free electricity, free road usage, free of all basic amenities, but if you want to live a life of luxury then you go into business, but when it comes to natural and national amenities everyone in this world should live well. As a result, you will find that crime would be minimal and killing and other atrocities would reduce. This is because those who were very rich in their previous life, but **the Supreme Nature** has subdued their nature this time; because of the way they treated people when they were rich before now. **I** have made them to become poor beggars, and they are not happy, so they go about as arm-robbers and thieves and committing other atrocities that are evil to gain a living because that spirit of living well is still within them. However, they do not know themselves, therefore if you help them to establish well, then you are helping the world and yourself in the time to come to be in peace. This is the **WORD** of **WISDOM** and **EQUALITY**. I had set a proper example in the United Kingdom by establishing equality and that means that in the history of the United Kingdom there is a spirit of practice called **EQUALITY** which is supposed to look after everyone.

The spirit of **EQUALITY** has manifested **THE WISDOM** of **GOD** and this is the **WORD** of **WISDOM**. As a summery, the **WORD** of **WISDOM** means that, every amenity which is national amenities of the whole world should be free and shared equally. Do not think that you have the right to live well and other people do not have the right to live well. Make a simple way of providing these amenities to everyone and then you will have **WISDOM** which makes you a house of **GOD** and a servant of **GOD**.

CONCLUSION TWO: FORMATION OF POSITIVE BEHAVIOURS

If you take care of everybody and do all the above then you are helping every human soul to behave well. You should look after your wife, so that if your wife goes about stealing and prostituting herself then you will know that she is really a bad woman, because condition can make some women to go and fornicate. However sometimes, if you trust your wife very well and keep unto her alone and she trust you, then she would also keep herself for you alone. **EVERYTHING TAKES EVERYTHING TO BECOME**

EVERYTHING and that is why **I** judge the course of things and not through what people say. If you are the course of a problem in the world then the punishment belongs to you.

Take the continent of Africa as an example. Look at a country like Nigeria and Ghana where **I** have buried so many resources such as gold, silver, aluminium, and oil and every resource that they can sufficiently share for Africa and the whole world. But now some of the evil corrupted African people are taking the African wealth wrongly to the people of the west because of greed rather than generating the riches of such resources among themselves and to everyone in the whole world, therefore what do you want **THE FATHER GOD** to do? And that is why **I AM** looking for a **MASTER, KING** or **SOMEONE** who would be able to put this **WORD** into action and bring **EQUALITY** to all mankind. If you **PROMISE ME** that you will do this then **I** will stand on your side until **MY** will comes to past. However, **I THE FATHER GOD** does not trust anyone apart from having spirit of love because in the whole world, people are evil and that is why **I** have come by **MYSELF** in **SPIRITUAL** ways. However, do not forget that this is comprehensive **MANUAL** and **GUIDE** to every ruler, every senior, every home, every chair person, every teacher, and to every person on **HOW TO SPEAK THE WORD, HOW TO MANIPULATE THE WORD, HOW TO ENGINEER THE WORD, HOW TO USE THE WORD TO CONTROL THE WORLD** and **HOW** to **HELP** people and rule with love, unity and peace. This is a **MANUAL** that you must apply in everything because anything outside of this makes you a wanted person. **I** have declared it! All spirits, all souls, and all principalities will war against evil practice of all kinds, because they all know about this teaching and this order. This **WORD** that **I AM TALKING** constitutes everything seen and unseen, heard and unheard, touchable and untouchable, therefore if you deviate from this order, then those things will revoke against you and do not blame anyone, even **GOD**, but blame yourself for purposely taking **VOLUNTARY EVOLUTION** to destroy your soul. However any soul that stands with this order from **G-O-D** and **G-O-C** is **BLESSED** and **NON STOP BLESSING** will follow you now and forevermore, *Amien.*

Let **MY** peace and blessing abide with the entire world now and forever more, *Amien*.

In the name of Our Lord Jesus Christ
In the blood of Our Lord Jesus Christ
Now and forever more, *Amien*

THANK YOU FATHER

Prayer of thanks by: **HRM QUEEN DISEM**

Let thanks and praises be given to **THE FATHER** in the name of Our Lord Jesus Christ, *Amien.*
Let thanks and praises be given to **THE FATHER GOD** in the blood of Our Lord Jesus Christ, *Amien.*
Let thanks and praises be given to **THE SUPREME FATHER WHO** has come to establish **THE WORD** and teach man **HOW TO SPEAK THE WORD** now and forevermore, *Amien*

HOLY, HOLY FATHER, thank **YOU** immensely for this wonderful day, the AO of AO, of **FATHER**, OG. Thank **YOU** for this supreme season of **THE WORD**, the season of all positivism. Thank **YOU FATHER** for this positive and progressive lecture on **HOW TO SPEAK THE WORD** and **USE THE WORD** and **DIVINE THE WORD** so that it would represent **YOU AS THE SUPREME WORD**. Thank **YOU FATHER OLUMBA OLUMBA OBU** for revealing the positive five stars as mercy love righteousness, kindness and peace so that through these virtues we will know how to speak well. If we are merciful we would speak well, if we have love we will speak well, if we practice righteousness we will speak well, if we are peaceful we will speak well, if we are kind we will also speak well and if we are peaceful then all these things will manifest well for all creation.

Thank **YOU FATHER** for giving us the instruction manual on **HOW TO USE THE WORD** for everybody in the entire universe, so as to have wisdom and understanding and think well, speak well and do well so that all will be well with all creation, thank **YOU FATHER** for coming to establish equality for all humankind, and to give us ability to always connect with **THY DIVINE SPIRIT** so that all will be well with us, now and forever, more, *Amien*.

Let thanks and praises be given to **THE FATHER** in the name of Our Lord Jesus Christ, *Amien.*
Let thanks and praises be given to **THE FATHER** in the blood of Our Lord Jesus Christ, *Amien.*
Let thanks and praises be given to **THE WISDOM ITSELF, THE FATHER GOD THE CREATOR OF THE UNIVERSE** who has come to reign supreme now and forever, more, *Amien.*

THANK YOU FATHER
=========

Chapter Two

THE MANUAL OF LIFE

(HOW TO LIVE THE POSITIVE LIFE)

FATHER'S TALK
(GOD PRESENT)

Date: BF/AO/OG (The twenty sixth day of the tenth moth of **THE FATHER** 'year' two thousand and seven).

In the name of Our Lord Jesus Christ, In the blood of Our Lord Jesus Christ, Now and forever more, *Amien*.

THE MANUAL OF LIFE
(HOW TO LIVE THE POSITIVE LIFE)

The Lecture Revelation this morning is on how to **LIVE LIFE**, titled **THE MANUAL OF LIFE**.

A: INTRODUCTION

It has pleased **ME, THE FATHER GOD THE CREATOR OF THE UNIVERSE** this morning to give this wonderful Lecture Revelation tilted **HOW TO LIVE LIFE, THE MANUAL OF LIFE**. Since the creation from the time of Adam and before that, **I** have never ever given man the **MANUAL OF LIVE**. Man has been in primary education to develop and reach the stage of perfection. As such, it would not be very good to give the instruction and **MANUAL** to someone who is still under training. The manufacturer produces a **MANUAL** on how to use any product when the process of testing has perfected the product. Now **I AM** selling **LIFE** out, **PERFECT LIFE, EVERLASTING LIFE, LOVE, PEACE, HARMONY,** and **PATIENCE** as the things that make **LIFE** meaningful in the spirit and in the truth physical world. **LIFE** is a spirit and **LIFE** means **GOD**. **LIFE** is **GOD HIMSELF**, as such; no human being on earth can engineer **LIFE**. You can only be a witness to the engineering of **LIFE** such as through healing in many ways such as being a doctor or doing one thing or the other to make **LIFE** meaningful on earth. No one, not even angels have the **POWER** to give the actual meaning of

LIFE which is a spirit. It is only **I THE FATHER GOD THE CREATOR OF THE UNIVERSE** that can give the meaning of **LIFE**, because **I AM LIFE** and that is why **I** have now brought the **MANUAL OF LIFE**. A week before this Lecture Revelation, **I** revealed the **MANUAL OF THE SPOKEN WORD** titled, **HOW TO SPEAK THE WORD** which is **THE MAKER** of **LIFE**, but this Lecture Revelation is to reveal **THE MANUAL OF LIFE** itself. **I AM TALKING** about **LIFE** in terms of having a **GOOD** character, but **THE WORD** is **LIFE** and since **I** have given the **MANUAL** of **THE WORD** as the introduction to **LIFE**, it means that **LIFE** has become permanent; therefore, man should have **THE MANUAL OF LIFE**. **THE WORD** is **THE CREATOR** therefore, it befits that **I** should give **THE MANUAL OF LIFE** after **THE MANUAL OF THE WORD** to all living creatures. This **MANUAL OF LIFE** is mainly for living creatures as human beings. All living creatures that have taken an evolution from other natures to mankind should have **THE MANUAL OF LIFE**. From the moment a woman conceives a baby in her womb, she should start reading **THE MANUAL OF THE WORD** and **THE MANUAL OF LIFE** to the foetus so that by the time the baby is born, he or she knows the type of **LIFE** that they are supposed to live. Indeed the type of **LIFE** that **I** permit everyone to live on this earth and every planet. **I** want to use this **MANUAL OF LIFE** to inform the entire universe and all creation, from spirit, soul, and physical truth human being, also angels that **I** have changed their gears, because this is the time of perfection and seriousness, hence **MY BUSINESS** has started. So far as you are a human being, spirit, soul, angel, good or evil or anyhow you may classify yourself, you must take this **MANUAL** as a code of conduct and a companion for living **LIFE** if you do not want to be a debtor to death and everlasting death. If you do anything other than

The Spiritual General Manual Of Life

the instructions that **I** have given in these **MANUALS**, then you have signed up to a voluntary evolution to death rather than **LIFE**. If you want your soul to live a perfect and everlasting **LIFE** then you must willingly accept and comply with this **MANUAL**. This is the instruction book of **LIFE** as the **MANUAL OF LIFE** on how to live a **GOOD** and **PERFECT LIFE** that has something to do with **ME, YOUR CREATOR, THE HOLY SPIRIT OF TRUTH**. This would be the authorised **LIFE** that **I** permit rather than the **LIFE** that you live as a wanted person, a coward and as one that is dead already. **I** have now given this introduction on how to live **LIFE** and no human being on earth or any other creation in any form is bigger than this Lecture Revelation. Every human being and living creature must adhere to this **MANUAL** unless you are not going to be **ALIVE** or you are not going to take an evolution into the **CONTINUATION SOUL WORLD OF**

LIFE. Whatever living nature that you think you have, you must use this **MANUAL** to live. If you have ten heads or a hundred heads or you call yourself Jehovah, or Emanuel or whatever that **GOD** had made you to be, this is your **MANUAL** on earth. You must read this **MANUAL** and accept it whole heartedly. From the time that you hear or read this **MANUAL**, you should know that things have changed and that **I** have **IMPROVED** to **THE PERFECTION CYCLE OF LIFE** and for all **CONTINUITY OF LIFE**. This **MANUAL OF CONTINUITY** will carry on from generation to generation for **ETERNITY** which is **ENDLESS**. **I** would base the **MANUAL OF LIFE** on **BELIEVING** and having **FAITH**. **I** would use this **MANUAL** to change the world. **I** will use this **MANUAL** to make things **GOOD** and **PERFECT** because all human beings in the world whether in the spirit, soul or physically, must use the instruction of this **MANUAL** to live. In any planet or sphere that you may live on, this **MANUAL** will guide you and you must comply and live according to the instructions within it and that is the introduction that **I** have today. This is **MY LIFE** that **I AM** exposing. **I AM THE FATHER GOD THE CREATOR OF THE UNIVERSE**, and **I** have decided to expose **MY INTEGRITY, MY DIGNITARY, MY LIFE** and **MY INNER SELF** so that you would know who **I AM** and what **I** want and how **MY LIFE** is linked to human beings as **LOVE** because **I AM LOVE**. **I** have not hid anything from you as **CHRIST** said, **I AND MY FATHER ARE ONE**, and that means that you, **MY CREATION**, and **I** your **FATHER**, is **ONE** today. In effect, we are one when we comply with this instruction and **MANUAL OF LIFE** in every situation.

(B) LIVING THE LIFE OF POSITIVISM

First, you all know that **THE LIFE OF THE FATHER GOD** is a **POSITIVE LIFE**. **I** know so many people take different forms to control things of this world. Some through angels, some through spirit soul or even through the dream world and so on and so forth, because they believe that **THE FATHER** is mixed with many things which is true, but **I** do not want to go much into all that at present. However, **MY POSITIVE** organ and **MY POSITIVE SELF** is **THE HOLY SPIRIT** and **MY** other **SELVES** were experimental stages. When you are doing experiments, you can do so many things because you may purposely create things as part of the experimental stage. After you have arrived at the final analyses of your experiment, you would produce the perfect product and condemn the rest. That is why the meaning of **GOD** or **LIFE** is not as people think.

Their thinking is that everything was created by **THE FATHER GOD** as such, they can mix with negativism, therefore, evil and demon believe that they are the creations of **GOD** and that **THE FATHER GOD** is part of those things, but that is null and void. **I** have disowned them outright. **THE SELF OF MINE** that **I** have designed and forwarded for everyone to live as **ME** is **POSITIVE, POSITIVE,** and **POSITIVE**. Everyone must live the **POSITIVE LIFE** and that is what this Lecture Revelation is all about and that is why **I** provide the **MANUAL** of how to live a **POSITIVE LIFE** and to a neat **LIVE LIFE** in general this day.

I have explained in so many Lectures Revelations that since **I EXIST**, as **THE EXISTENCE**, **I** was **BEEN** as **BEING** and **I WAS, WAS, WAS**, but being that **I AM LOVE, I** made **MY** singular to become plural. **I** singularly made **MYSELF PLURAL** as **PLURALISM** which is you, man, woman, animal, bird, fish, tree, flowers, water, air, sand, fruits, vegetables, seeds and any other thing that you can imagine both in spirit, the soul and in the physical as natural, spiritual and otherwise. It is the spirit of **LOVE** that **I** used to make **MYSELF** to become **PLURAL**. **I** did not become **PLURAL** so that people and other creatures would be wicked to each other. Anyone who practices wickedness is a spiritual baby at an elementary stage of **LIFE**. When you are involved in an experimental programme or writing a report, or essay and creating anything, you will edit and take away the parts which you no longer need. These parts are the elementary spirits that are demons and evil. For example, during the process of developing this Lecture Revelation, **I** will edit the sprinter of spit that came into this Lecture Revelation. **I** will correct all the past tense, the present future as the grammar, spelling errors and other errors so that it would be suited for the purpose for which **I** produced it, which is to be read and understood by human beings who want to live well. The edited out parts, through the process of making corrections would become negative as, demons and as things that you would not like to re use in this Lecture Revelation. If you go and put the edited parts back after **I** have produced and signed off the final copy then you are an idiot! You are trading with a baby spirit because you want to go back to something that has passed and that is what people do. They would say that **THE FATHER** is this and that thereby going back to use elementary knowledge that **I** have used as an experiment and moved on from that stage. They burn candles, incense, invoking demons, calling angels and sacrificing for idols and doing rituals to command all sorts of things practising evil. They excuse themselves by saying that other people have done it before, but who are these people? It was Satan and other evil people therefore; **I** have no hand in that. Anything that people do in connection to sacrificing to idols, rituals in any way such as sprinkling blood, going to the tree, the water, to the sun to do some ritual, and any other such incantations have nothing to do with **ME, THE PERSONIFIED HOLY SPIRIT OF TRUTH**. **I** will tell you what **MY LIFE** is and the **LIFE** that **I** authorise for everyone to live everywhere, here and there. **I** have nothing to do with candles or incense in the name of invocation. You can light a candle to see where you are going. You can prepare food such as fruits and vegetables and seeds to eat which are the foods for the perfect living **LIFE**, but not to use them for rituals. You can eat anything that will not intoxicate or harm you or another person. You are not to eat any flesh or blood. In short, no one should eat anything that is flesh and blood that lives because when you eat life, you are injecting another **LIFE** into **LIFE**. You can eat living organisms such as herbs that **I** have created for eating that work through the blood. These are the body of **CHRIST** as the body of **THE WORD**. These are the pop up sands such as rice, beans, and all fruits that grow in the ground and the ones that grow up in the air. The upper fruits such as mango, oranges, (pawpaw) papaya, pineapple, bananas and all the other fruits that are in the air are those that when you eat, helps the spirit in you to grow in the divine positive way. These are better than the pop up sands that grow in the ground such as cassava, yam, potatoes and others that grow in the soil because when you eat too much of them it brings you down. If you want to be more spirited and **THINK WELL**, **SPEAK WELL** and **DO WELL** then you must mostly eat, the pop up foods of the body of **CHRIST** that grows in the air. The reason that the nature has brought some foods to gel up in the air, such as coconuts, plantains, and many others, is because these fruits, vegetables, seeds and herbs, are improved foods from the sand up. When you eat them, it helps you to develop spiritually than those that grow in the soil. For instance, if you eat plantain, it is better than eating yams because yam is the heavy sand and it would take you downwards where as plantain and others that grow in the air would take you upwards. Vegetables give blood and such provide energy to the body. This is the way you should feed in this physical world. These are the things that would help you to have a quality of life in the spirit of **THE FATHER GOD**, because **THE LIFE OF GOD** is a **POSITIVE LIFE** and negativism has nothing to do with it. Take away sacrificing, worshiping idols, making incantations and all other negative practices such invocations, magic and rituals etc, etc. And anything such as invoking ghosts after someone has died to come to help you is unacceptable. The only ghost that you are permitted to call is that of **CHRIST**, the personified **SUPREME**

WORD GHOST, OUR LORD JESUS CHRIST. I AM not interested in any other thing than that. If you call the spirit of Our Lord Jesus Christ to help you then that is fine because that is **ME** in **THE HOLY GHOST**. The only **HOLY GHOST** that man can call is **THE SPIRIT OF CHRIST** and you should not call anything more than that because if you do, you are in trouble with evil spirits souls. **I** do not permit you to call your father or your mother or your child or any other relative who has died to come and help you because when you do that, you are making an incantation to imperfect ghosts. The **HOLY GHOST** is through the name of Our Lord Jesus Christ and if you do not like to call the name of Our Lord Jesus Christ then you are in trouble with **ME THE PERSONIFIED HOLY SPIRIT OF TRUTH**. The only invocation name that you need to call is **OOO** through the Name and Blood of Our Lord Jesus the Christ. If you say, in the name of Our Lord Jesus Christ, through the blood of Our Lord Jesus Christ, **OOO** then all is well. **OOO** means **GOD** of the **HEAVEN**, **GOD** of the **SOUL** and **GOD** of **EARTH**. If you invoke that name then **I THE HOLY SPIRIT OF GOD, THE CREATOR OF THE UNIVERSE** will help you. Anything other than this is elementary which is evil and **I** do not permit you to call any old master, any angel and any person. If you consult these spirits, you are reducing yourself to those backward spirits. If you want to improve your life then this is the only way to go about it.

When you have this **MANUAL** and follow the **INSTRUCTIONS**, no one can harm you because you are not under anyone again. Even the secret societies that they establish all over the world to control people cannot control you once you have **THE MANUAL OF LIFE** and follow it. You are under **THE SUPREME BEING** which is **THE ALMIGHTY FATHER GOD, THE GOD OF ALL CREATION**.

When you **BELIEVE** this, **I** would elevate your spirit above all things and you will live the **LIFE OF GOD**, therefore this **MANUAL OF LIFE** becomes your open society. This **MANUAL** would become everything for you. It would become your **PROTECTION**, your **GUIDE**, and **INSURANCE** and give you **MAXIMUM SECURITY**. **BELIEVE** it because no one can harm your and this is the only way that your soul can survive for eternity without subjecting yourself to anything negative. Throw away all talismans, rings as a form of spiritual connection and books from all old masters that teach you elementary practices. Evil books bring about evil dreams because reading is communication. If you read any book that people publish, through whatever spirit soul that lives in the author, then you connect yourself to those elementary spirit-souls. From therein, you will be seeing them turn themselves into objects that come and fight against you or fight someone around you without even your knowledge and people will start to call you a wizard and witch.

Now **I** have set everybody free. If you read from **ME THE FATHER** as **GOD'S INSTRUCTION** from **THE FATHERS TALK** through **THE SUPER HOLY SPIRIT, THE ALMIGHTY GOD**, and **THE DIVINE WISDOM** which does not require any ceremony, then you are free. You do not need to light a candle or use incense or perform any other act than to read the **MANUAL OF LIFE** and **BELIEVE** that it is **THE SPOKEN WORD, ME** your **CREATOR** then you are free. **I** have set every soul **FREE FOR ETERNITY**. When you believe in **ME THE FATHER GOD ALMIGHTY** then you are in **THE SCHOOL OF THE HIGHER SELF, BROTHERHOOD MASTERSHIP**. Read all the Lecture Revelation from King Solomon's Spiritual Library and you will grow in **UNDERSTANDING** and all will be well with your spirit, soul, and your natural system. **WHERE THE SPIRIT OF THE LORD IS, THERE IS LIBERTY** and **THIS IS MY SPIRIT, MY TRUTH** and **MY TRUE SELF, THE HOLY SPIRIT**. As **I AM TALKING** now through HRM King Solomon **ETE**, **I** have checked him completely and he has nothing to do with any incantation. He desires and accepts to be a **POSITIVE** child of **THE FATHER GOD**. And for this reason, when you read this book, do not say, oh but **I** have more wisdom that this, **I** can write better English than this, **I** know more things than this, **I** have written more books than this etc, etc. This Lecture Revelation has nothing to do with all that. It has something to do with where the Lecture Revelation came from which is **THE LINK TO AND FROM THE FATHER GOD**. It has nothing to do with knowledge rather it is about **SPIRITUAL WISDOM** and who sends whom and who directs whom and who possesses whom.

What spirit did you use to write your book? Who authorised you to write those books, therefore throw all your knowledge and wisdom away and embrace this one because this **SUPERSEDES** all of them. This **WISDOM** bypasses all others and it is from **ME THE FATHER GOD ALMIGHTY THE UNIVERSAL SUPREME WORD**, therefore **I** have designed it with a **POTENCY** that would help every soul. From this basis, you must live a **POSITIVE LIFE** of **GOD WITH MY HOLY FORCE "HOLY GHOST"**. You should throw away all incantations and disbelieve everything negative such as witchcraft, freemasons and any other secret societies and others that **I** do not want to mention, but you know all of them. Those who have entered these things because of money, protection or for any other reason know what **I** mean. When you read this **MANUAL**, throw away all those things and they will not harm you. They would not even see you because

THE POWER OF GOD, MY DIVINE SELF SUPREME ENERGY from this reading would cover you with the supreme blood of **CHRIST**. And you have **THE HOLY SPIRIT** to call which **I** said in **MY** Divine Directive of communication with **ME THE FATHER GOD ALMIGHTY, THE PERSONIFIED HOLY TRINITY IN ONE SUPER SYSTEM** as "In the Name of Our Jesus **CHRIST**, In the Blood of Our Lord Jesus **CHRIST**, Now and forever more, then CALL **OOO**" and if you do this three times then you are free from all evil. This is the **PERFECT LIFE** that would carry on for eternity and that is **THE POSITIVE LIFE** that you must live from today. Every child, adult, man, woman, president, head of state, governor, local leaders, kings and queens, masters and servants and every other position must live this **LIFE**, as the **POSITIVE LIFE**. You must live the **LIFE** that has nothing to do with any evil such as hatred, jealousy and strife, telling lies about anyone rather you should live by the principle of '**live and let live**' which is the key of this **LIFE**. You should live the **LIFE** that makes you free and everyone else also free to live. You should **THINK WELL** and **PLAN WELL** for people. You should use this **LIFE** to think about what you can do to benefit each other. If you live any **LIFE** that would make someone sad or will bring problems to another person then that means that you have executed yourself away from this earth and your name would be in the hell fire. However, if you live the **LIFE** that encourages people to be **GOOD** and for things to be **GOOD** in the whole world, making **PEACE** and encouraging people to be **PEACEFUL**, **RESPECTING** each other and doing other **POSITIVE** things then, **I** shall place you among the saved list. Everybody knows what is **POSITIVE** and what is negative, therefore throw away the negative things and practice **POSITIVISM**. This is the type of

LIFE that **I** expect everyone to **LIVE** from now up forever and no one is bigger than this type of **LIFE**. If you do otherwise, **I** will subdue you to dust which is worst than serpent.

C: **THE HOLY LIFE OF GOD**

After you have thrown away all negativism then the next stage is to live a **HOLY LIFE OF GOD.** By now, you should know the meaning of **GOD. GOD** means **GOOD. A GOOD** nature, **GOOD** atmosphere, **GOOD** environment, **GOOD** self, **GOOD WORD, GOOD THINKING, GOOD SPEAKING** and **GOOD DOING.** By **THINKING WELL, SPEAKING WELL** and **HEARING WELL, SEEING WELL** and **DOING WELL** you are living the **GOOD LIFE**, as **THE LIFE OF GOD.** Some people claim that they do not believe in **GOD**, but you **BELIEVE** in **GOODNESS.** You say, **GOODNESS** me, my **GOOD** father, my **GOOD** friend, my **GOOD** sister, my **GOOD** mother, my **GOOD** brother, my

GOOD manager, my **GOOD** co-workers, my **GOOD** chairperson, my **GOOD** president, my **GOOD** king, my **GOOD** queen, my **GOOD** preacher, my **GOOD LIFE**, Oh **GOODNESS** me! Why do you not happily proclaim your bad friend or your own bad manner, a bad sister and a bad brother, a bad mother and a bad father, and so forth? You are happy to have **GOODNESS** from others, and all this **GOODNESS** means **GOD** as the nature of a **GOOD Life**.

This is **THE LIFE MANUAL OF GOOD LIFE** that every living creature and every living human must live from generation to generation. When you sign up to this **LIFE MANUAL**, you are signing on to **PERFECTION** and you are signing up to **LIVE WELL**. However, if you resign from this, then you are a wanted and dead person and your **SOUL** and your blood would be upon you, because you now know that this is the **LIFE LIVING MANUAL** on how to live a **POSITIVE**

The Spiritual General Manual Of Life

PERFECT and **GODLY LIFE** on earth. **I** do not permit anyone to go to war. **I** do not permit any human being to fight or harm another human being. **I** do not permit anyone to steal other people things as arm robbers by carrying guns and any other weapons and waste lives. **I** do not permit anyone to create any deadly instrument of any kind that would kill another human being. **I** do not permit anyone to produce food or drink or drugs of any kind that would bring harm to a human being. If you create any of these things knowing full well that it could harm people, but carry on because of wanting to make money, then you are evil and are condemning your soul and **I** would seek the blood of those people from your hand. This world is going to be **PEACEFUL** and nothing evil would exist again in this world.

People may not **BELIEVE** that **I** could not do otherwise until now, but today, **I** have created the **MANUAL OF**

LIVE, therefore, if you live a different **LIFE** than this, it means that you have taken a voluntary evolution to be ceased from **LIFE**. If you do not accept this **MANUAL OF LIFE**, it means that you have automatically ceased yourself from **LIFE** for eternity and you can no more be found because you have signed away from positive **LIFE**, therefore you are not in **LIFE**. However if you sign on to this **MANUAL OF LIFE**, then you have signed in to **LIFE** as the **LIFE** of **DIVINE GOD**. **MY LIFE** is the **PERFECT LIFE**, because it is **LOVE, PEACE, KINDNESS, UNITY, EQUALITY, JOY, HARMONY, MERCY, TEMPERANCE,** and **PATIENCE**. The **LIFE** of **GOD** is that you should have **LOVE** and **PATIENCE** in everything that you do. You must consider the **LIFE** of **GOD**, which is the **LIFE** of **GOODNESS** in whatever that you do in this world. You should be **GOOD** in your nature. Do not accept anything that harms someone and do not accept any human being that hates another human being. If you have a mother, father, brother sister, friend or any other type of relationship with anyone that hates somebody, excommunicate yourself from such an individual. Do not have anything to do with such a person because such a person has rejected **LIFE** as such **LIFE** has ceased from them and their blood would be upon them no matter who they are.

You know that the **TRUTH** remains **TRUTH**. Do not ask where this information came from or where this voice comes from. This is not the voice of anyone; it is the **WORD** of **GOD**, **THE FATHER'S TALK** and **THE SPOKEN WORD** and it is a **POSITIVE WORD**, a **PERFECT** and **BLESSED WORD**. You are to take **THE WORD** because when you accept this **WORD** and practice it, it means you have accepted **ME THE FATHER GOD** and by accepting **ME THE FATHER GOD**, you accept

POSITIVISM thereby accepting **LIFE**.

If someone cooks a nice meal for you that is blessed, would you keep asking who prepared it? What is the essence of asking who prepared the food? If you do not want to eat the food then remain hungry. **I** have cooked a meal for you which is **THE FOOD OF LIFE**. This **WORD** is **LIFE ITSELF**. **THE MANUAL OF LIFE** is **LIFE**. If everyone lives, their **LIFE** by this **MANUAL** then there would be **PERFECT PEACE** everywhere, here and there which means that the Kingdom of **GOD** has established in reality and in practice rather than in theory where everyone in the world is shouting *kingdom of GOD*, *kingdom of GOD*, but it is all with their lips and not in reality through their practical manners. You tell people that you are in the kingdom of **GOD**, but you hate people and destroy people's reputation by assassinating their character; you practice witchcraft, go to soothsayers and involve yourself in all sorts of negative things. By doing any of these things, you are not in the kingdom of **GOD** and you are deceiving people by going about broadcasting that you are in the kingdom of **GOD**. All the people that are involved in these negative practices have resigned themselves away from **LIFE**. However if you are **TRUTHFUL** and what you **THINK**, **SPEAK, SEE, HEAR** and **DO** are the same then you are with **ME THE FATHER GOD** wherever you be and live and **I THE FATHER GOD** can never disappoint you. "**IN MY NAME OF THE ENTIRETY OF MY EXISTENCE, I AM THAT I AM, THE FATHER GOD ALMIGHTY, THE CREATOR OF UNIVERSE, THE UNIVERSAL SUPREME WORD, THE SPOKEN WORD, I** will back you if you back **YOURSELF** with this **MANUAL**. If you **ACCEPT** this **MANUAL, I** will **ACCEPT** you. If you **ACCEPT** this **WORD** then **I** will stand by your soul and your spirit. And if anyone comes to raise his or her head to give you any type of trouble, this **WORD** and **I** would deal with that person. For all the people that have assigned to **ACCEPT** this **TRUTH**, the **TRUTH** will **ACCEPT** them and guide them and become their protection and everything of everything for them. However, if you deny this **WORD**, this **WORD** would deny you and that means that you are no more because you have ceased to exist. **LET THE WHOLE LIFE OF ALL LIFE OF TOTALITY OF MY DIVINE FORCES BACK THOSE WHO ACCEPT AND USE THIS LIFE MANUAL BECAUSE IT IS THE PRACTICE THAT WOULD ENDURE FOR ETERNITY**, in the Name and the Blood of Our Lord Jesus Christ, *Amien!*

I do not need to continue to **TALK** too much about **THE LIFE OF GOOD** as **THE LIFE OF GOD** because if you are a **GOOD** person, you know what is **GOOD**. As soon as you sign on to use this **LIFE MANUAL**, you will know what is **GOOD**, because **I AM THE SPIRIT** of **thought as the silent thought** in you. **I** will gel the fruit of **GOOD** thought in you which would lead you to **THINK WELL, SPEAK WELL, SEE WELL, HEAR WELL** and that would manifest **DOING WELL**. And that means that you have become a soul that would be living with **ME THE FATHER GOD** for eternity. You will become an instrument of **THE GLORY OF GOD**. Your soul and name will inherit the kingdom of **GOD**. This is **THE LIFE OF GOD**, because there is nothing like **GOD** apart from **GOOD** and there is nothing **LIKE GOOD** apart from **ME THE FATHER GOD**. If you have a **GOOD** heart and are a **GOOD** person, you will **THINK WELL** and **DO WELL**, but if on the other hand, you are an evil person, you will think evil and speak evil. And for this reason, you must be on the **GOOD** side and you will do **GOOD** things, but if you are on the other side and practice evil, then that is up to you from now upward.

D: THE TWELVE CHARACTERISTICS OF THE HOLY SPIRIT OF TRUTH.

The **TWELVE CHARACTERS** of **THE HOLY SPIRIT** are the **PILLARS** of **LIFE**. Each of the **TWELVE** (AB) **CHARACTERS** has seventy two (GB) million **POSITIVE SELVES** as children that are **PEACE, LOVE, MERCY, LIFE, FAITH, TRUTH UNDERSTANDING, WISDOM, RIGHTEOUSNESS, KINDNESS, JOY, HOPE** and so on and so forth. When you have **LOVE** and **FAITH**, you will be **PEACEFUL, MERCIFUL** and you will have **PATIENCE** and **HOPE** and **UNDERSTANDING** and that would automatically materialise **WISDOM**. And **WISDOM** is **THE HOLY SPIRIT** in you. When you have all these **GOOD CHARACTERS OF THE FATHER GOD** in you, your **LIFE** becomes permanently **PEACEFUL**. You will become an environment of **GOOD LIFE** for people.

For instance, people desire to live in areas that there are no problems. They like peaceful areas where people are not involved in fights and arguments and are generally behaving well. People want to live in an area where there is no crime, no arm robbers, shooting of people, drug use and all sorts of negative practices. Everybody wants to live in a **PEACEFUL** area where people are not killing themselves. To this end, wealthy people who can afford to do so buy Islands where crime does not exist and there is serenity to spend time there. They put security in place so that before you can go there, they first check you thoroughly. Why do you want to do that? It is because you do not want trouble and you do not want to die, therefore you must know that **IN MY OWN WORLD, THE ENTIRE UNIVERSE, I, DO NOT WANT TROUBLE**! **I** do not want anyone to manufacture drugs that harm people. **I** do not want anyone to manufacture weapons that are for use in harming people. **I** do not want scientist or manufacturers of any technology to create anything for the use of harming or destroying **LIFE**. If you do any of these, you are a wanted person. **I** have put security in all aspects of **LIFE**; therefore anyone that is involved in these things should immediately cease from such practice or face the consequences.

Some of the twelve **FRUITS OF THE HOLY SPIRIT** is **JOY, HAPPINESS, GOOD ZEAL**, and **IMAGINATION OF GOOD** things and an **INSPIRATION** of **GOOD** things. Therefore, be **INSPIRED** to build roads for people, to give electrify, water and all other things that make **LIFE** comfortable, free of charge. Be **INSPIRED** to make the whole world one so that everyone would live in **PEACE**. Be **INSPIRED** to use this **MANUAL OF LIFE** and the other **MANUALS** on **HOW TO SPEAK THE WORD**, to change the whole world. If you are a good king and queen, president, prime minister, head of state, a good governor, chairperson or in any position of responsibility, through the will of **THE FATHER GOD**, use all the **MANUALS** to rule the office that you head. If you do this, you and **ME THE FATHER GOD** can be friends and your **MIND** will be at rest, because you will be happy that you are doing what is **GOOD**. Exception of this, you are in trouble whether you believe it or not. By now you know that **THE WORD** is **GOD** therefore, **THE WORD** is everything, if you did not know previously. And this **WORD**, as **THE GOOD WORD** and **THE GOOD SPIRIT** wants to rule. This is **THE TIME OF GOD**. When **I** talk about **GOD RULING** the whole world, it is through **THE POSITIVE WORD**, because **GOD** is not going to come as a human being and start using force to rule you. If you practice what is **GOOD** then **GOD** rules you Life, if your house is in **PEACE**, **GOD** rules you, if you are heading any office and all your people are **HAPPY**, because you treat them well then **GOD** is ruling you. **GOOD** means **GOD**, **HAPPINESS** means **GOD**, **PEACE** means **GOD**, **PATIENCE** means **GOD**, **JOY** means **GOD** and all **POSITIVISM'S** means **GOD**, therefore when you are established with all these things then automatically, **GOD** is ruling you.

Where you see fighting, arrogance, jealousy, strife, killing and wickedness of all forms, then it is Satan that is ruling that place. When you see a president or prime minister or head of state or church leader who permits a man to marry another man, or woman to marry another woman then you must ask yourself who is ruling such a person, because these are abominations that **I** do not permit in the kingdom of **GOD** and in the whole wide world. **THINGS MUST WORK WELL**. When you see people manufacture arms such as nuclear weapons, guns, jet fighters, bombs and all sorts of things to go about killing others, it means that it is Satan that is ruling them. Nuclear energy is supposed to generate power to provide electricity and other things that would help people rather, you use it to go about killing people. All those involved in these practices are wanted souls. If you create drugs that make people not to behave well, you are wanted person. Some people are born fine, but when they start to use narcotics, they start to walk about on the streets without a sense of what they are about and their life becomes a mess then if you are a part of the process of their difficulties in any way then you shall pay for it! When you do rituals and all sorts of things to kill people and manipulate people and mess up their life's rendering them useless, you will pay for it, no matter what you may be, because you know what you are doing! **I** have said this time without number and **THE WORD** shall come to pass. If **THE WORD** is **GOD** and it is **EVERYTHING** then do not think that any of **THE FATHER'S TALK WORD** shall not come to pass. Whether you believe it or not, one day you will see it operating in you. You know that it is not the same time that you plant a seed that it germinates, because it will take a while to come out and that is how this **WORD** will also take a while. However, it must surely come to pass either **POSITIVELY** or negatively depending on which side you chose to use in your operations with people. If you refuse to adhere to this **WORD** and take the negative side, the negative consequence would befall you however if choose the **POSITIVE** side then equally you will receive a **POSITIVE** outcome and that is **THE FATHER'S** judgement.

All the characteristics of **GOODNESS** are in this **MANUAL**. Use this **MANUAL** to create **GOOD** relationships with others. Be a **GOOD** mother, a **GOOD** father, a **GOOD** child, a **GOOD** husband, a **GOOD** wife, a **GOOD** chairperson, a **GOOD** manager, a **GOOD** director, a **GOOD** president, a **GOOD** minister, a **GOOD** preacher, a **GOOD** king, a **GOOD** queen and a **GOOD** leader in everything. If you have adopted **MY CHARACTERS**, then you are a servant of **GOD** to rule according to **MY** directives and **I, THE FATHER GOD, THE CREATOR OF THE UNIVERSE** will direct you all the time. These **MANUALS** are the **MANUALS** of rulership in the entire universe. Even unseen objects must use this **MANUAL** to operate. **THE WORD** is a **SPIRIT, THE WORD** is the **SOUL** and **THE WORD** is **PHYSICAL**, therefore all spirits souls, souls and physical things would use this **WORD** to manage every area in **LIFE**. You should know the **CHARACTERS** that are **GOOD** and base yourself on that. **LOVE, MERCY, KINDNESS, FAITH, UNDERSTANDING, WISDOM, PATIENCE, HAPPINESS, ZEAL**, and **IMAGINATION OF ALL GOOD**

THINGS, **LIFE** and all other **GOOD CHARACTERISTICS** are all **MY** attributes of **GOOD LIFE** of **THE SUPREME WORD** to direct you and do everything, and that is what **I** permit.

E: **PERFECT AND HOLY LIFE BRINGS PEACE ON EARTH**

If all of these **GOOD CHARACTERISTICS** of **GOD** are practised by human beings through this **MANUAL** of instructions or from the Holy Bible, the Holy Quran and other religious guide books then there would be no problems in the world. If you read the Holy Quran well, you will see the instructions from this **MANUAL** there. If you read the Bible very well, you will see that this instruction is there. If you read the Torah or the Tipitaka or other instructive religious doctrines, you will find this **INSTRUCTION**. There is no religious book that says that you should hate people or practice evil. **I** have instructed in different ways through all the inspirational books from **ME THE FATHER GOD** that people should **LOVE** each other, do what is **GOOD**, should not commit adultery and fornication, should not steal, should not make someone to feel bad and everybody knows that **LOVE** does not cause any problem. **I** do not mean **LOVE** of a man and a woman, **I** mean the charitable **LOVE**. **I** mean **LOVE** of **GOD** and the **LOVE** of tolerance. The **INSPIRATIONAL LOVE** that makes you do what is **GOOD** for everybody. With **LOVE, PEACE, JOY, GOOD WORD**, from **GOOD THINKING, GOOD SPEAKING, GOOD IDEALS, GOOD PLANNING**, a clean environment and every **GOOD** thing that you see would make the world to be **PERFECT** and **GOOD**. **I** have established this cite today in this **MANUAL** therefore this is the proper **MANUAL OF LIFE**. It is about how to **LIVE LIFE** for **LIFE** living brethren of **GOD** from today onwards for eternity.

The Spiritual General Manual Of Life

I want the entire world to be in **PEACE**. If a family uses this **MANUAL**, they would be in **PEACE**, if a state uses this **MANUAL**; they would be in **PEACE**, if a country uses this **MANUAL** they would be in **PEACE** and if the entire world uses this **MANUAL** the whole world will be in **PERFECT PEACE**. If you as an individual or any corporation or group use this **MANUAL**, you and they will be in **PERFECT PEACE** and everyone would enjoy a **PEACEFUL** world. Blessed are those who are going to hearken to this instruction so as to help the world to be in **PERFECT PEACE**. The servant of **GOD** means those who are using this **MANUAL** to transform their locality and the world, but first you must, transform yourself. When you transform your heart, then you can transform you sister, your children, your family and your neighbours. If after someone has had access to these **MANUALS**, but he or she refuses to adhere to it, then leave that person alone, because they are a wicked person and they would cease to exist. If you reject this **MANUAL**, you have rejected **LIFE**. Use an analogy of someone that purchases a car and rejects the **MANUAL** of driving. You should leave that person alone because they are already dead as when they get in the car and start the engine and drive without knowing the **MANUAL** of driving then that person is highly likely to crash. When you crash, you either destroy your car or yourself and others who associate with you. <u>This **MANUAL** means **LIFE** to you as a **SPIRITUAL LIFE** fire extinguisher and **LIFE** everlasting</u>. Even if someone is about to die today and he or she takes this **MANUAL** then he or she can come back to **LIFE**. If you reject it, you have automatically rejected **LIFE** and every **GOOD** thing that accompanies the living of **LIFE**.

There is no one that is bigger than this **MANUAL** as **I** have stated. Your duty is to help to spread the news about this **MANUAL**. You are to acquire it and spread it around by giving it to your children, your friends, and your community and so on and so forth. You can sponsor it and give to others as a gift. You must spread this **MANUAL** to the whole world. If you are expecting a child, keep a copy for that child and as soon as they are born, they should have a copy. You must start reading for that child whilst he or she is in your womb so that the child would be born with an acceptance of this **MANUAL**. **I** said that **I** would make everything new and now everything is new and that is what will camera and imprint in physical practice. The host of heaven in all **POSITIVE GOODNESS** is here and they would materialise physically as the **MANUAL** has come.

This **MANUAL** is brought to everyone on earth, to the governments, churches, mosques, other religious centres, regions, families and individuals so that **LIFE** would be **PEACEFUL** everywhere, here and there for all generations. Be you a Muslim, Christian, Buddhist, Jew, Hindu and all other religions of this world, Abraham, through Adam is the father of every human being on earth irrespective of your attachment to any religion or not. Our Lord Jesus Christ is the spiritual incarnate Father Adam, the second **PERSONIFIED WORD**, which was the same natural Father Abraham therefore Ishmael and Isaac are both from Abraham, therefore we all have one parent and we are all brethren and it does not matter what religion that you are or not. Anyone that hates another person in the name of religion or any for any reason will cease to exist. This **MANUAL** is to unite the whole world together, irrespective of religious affiliation or not. This **MANUAL** belongs to Christians, Muslims, Buddhist, Jews, Hindus, Sikhs and all other religions including those who do not affiliate to a particular religion. This **MANUAL** indeed belongs to all human beings, and anyone that is alive. If you reject this **MANUAL** then you have taken voluntary rejection of your **LIFE** and your blood would be upon you.

F: **THE LIFE OF UNDERSTANDING**

At this stage, there is **PERFECT PEACE** on earth through **PERFECT LIFE, LOVE, PATIENCE, TOLERANCE** and the practice of all **GOOD** things that **I** have spoken about today. No one should kill anyone or plan evil or use tradition to suppress people. From today there should not be any tradition existing in the whole world. There is no other tradition again except the tradition of the Universal Brotherhood of the same Parent, **THE FATHER GOD ALMIGHTY**. Brotherhood means a family of the same parent. This is **THE FATHER'S TRADITION** and **THE HOLY SPIRIT TRADITION**. It is now the tradition of **LOVE** and the tradition of **ONENESS** therefore all your formulated traditions have no bases from this moment. This is the new commandment, the new covenant of **GOD** that ye should **LOVE** one another. If you **LOVE** one another, you will not bring any tradition to harm anyone. This **MANUAL** has now nullified all the traditions that people used evil and lowerself to create and establish before now, because this supersedes all traditions. Do not plan any wicked act against anyone; do not cause division or segregation, do not hate anyone, do not strife rather there should be oneness in the world with one **FATHER** and one **MOTHER** and one brethren and that is the tradition that should be established in the whole world. The reason that **I** say that people should be careful about who they marry is because if you are a **GOOD** person and you marry a bad person then you are in trouble. However, when everyone is **OK** and has **LOVE** for one another and both Solid Skin and Soft Skin (Black and White) genuinely **LOVE** each other then you can inter-marry anyone because everyone would have the same template now through practicing of **LOVE**. **I AM** therefore using this **FATHER'S TALK** (**GOD PRESENT**) to teach you to **LOVE** so that there would be unity among all human beings and everyone would have the same template. However, if you are an offspring of human animals, the adulterers, the wicked people, and the people that adulterate **GOD'S** system then you cannot inter-marry with a human **GOD**. What is the meaning of adultery? Adultery means when Lucifer decided to spoil the programme of **GOD**, she went about adulterating things and the system of **GOD**. Adultery means adulteration of a system. If for instance, someone practices **LOVE** and as a result, their family is very loving and peaceful then you go and plant the seed of discord and segregation among them, you have committed adultery within that family. If you see, nice clean water and you drop specs of red liquid into that water, you have adulterated it. Some evil men go about sleeping with women so that they can put their evil blood in them. Some men sleep with women when they want to join a secret society by using mystical means. They go about sleeping with as many women as they can so that they can capture and spoil the star of these women. Some women that mermaids are directing use the spit of dragon to spoil the star of a man who fornicates with them and that is another form of adultery.

When you know that, someone's wife is happy, but you go and commit adultery with the woman so that you would spoil a happy home, then that is the meaning of adultery. It means by bringing a different system to spoil something. Everybody commits adultery with **ME** in this world. You know that **I AM THE FATHER GOD**,

THE GOOD SELF, GOOD SPIRIT, SPIRIT OF PEACE, SPIRIT OF LOVE and the **SPIRIT OF HARMONY**. I want **PERFECT PEACE** and for people to be happy, but you plant evil on earth and commit sin, cause segregation, cause confusion, hate people, deceive people and you generally make life difficult for children of **GOD**. You do not practice equality by sharing the amenities of **GOD** equally to everyone in the world and that means that you commit adultery against **ME**. This is the meaning of adultery. You also fornicate by performing rituals, by invocation, sacrificing, eating flesh and meat of any living creature and doing all sorts of things that are not **GOOD** and you shall face the judgement. However you can be set free if from the day that you have access to this **MANUAL** you start practicing what is **GOOD**. You allow people to be in **PEACE**, you practice **LOVE** for **ONE ANOTHER** which is the only commandment that **I** give now to the entire universe. Our Lord Jesus Christ introduced this commandment of **THE FATHER GOD** as the **REDEEMER** of the whole world and as **THE UNIVERSAL SUPREME SPOKEN WORD MANIFEST**. He introduced this **LOVE** and **I** have come today to sanction it and make this world to know that the only entity and **SPIRIT** that can rule the world successfully for everyone to be happy and have **PEACE** is **LOVE** and that is **ONENESS** which would bring **PERFECTION IN UNITY WITH ALL CREATIONS**. If you practice this, then you are **FREE** now and would be **FREE** forever. If you **LOVE ONE ANOTHER** that would bring **PEACE** and **JOY** and every other **GOOD** thing into the whole world. If from today, you accept this teaching, accept to **LOVE**, accept to be **HUMBLE**, accept to **THINK WELL**, accept to **SPEAK WELL**, accept to **SEE WELL**, accept to **HEAR WELL** and **DO WELL** then the world would change for **PEACE** and for **GOOD**. And if this spirit of

ONENESS governs the whole world then all would be **WELL** with you and your soul in the name of Our Lord Jesus Christ, *Amien*.

If you and your family become **PEACEFUL** then **UNDERSTANDING** has established in the whole world. If you have **UNDERSTANDING** and your **FAMILY** has **UNDERSTANDING**, then there would be **UNDERSTANDING** in your country and all endeavours of **LIFE** would have **UNDERSTANDING**. And through this **UNDERSTANDING**, **LIFE** would become easy and **PERFECT** in the whole world. From here, you can move on to the next stage.

G: **THE LIFE OF WISDOM**

The **LIFE** of **WISDOM** is a result of **UNDERSTANDING OF LIFE**. You establish with **WISDOM** if you have **UNDERSTANDING**. When you **UNDERSTAND** one another, there is

The Spiritual General Manual Of Life

PEACE and that is **WISDOM**. The **LIFE** of **WISDOM** also brings **UNDERSTANDING**. When you have **WISDOM**, you would **UNDERSTAND** your **LIFE** then through this **UNDERSTANDING**, the **WISDOM OF GOD** would come closer to you. **I** have revealed in other Lectures Revelations that the meaning of **WISDOM** is the wide angle of **THE FATHER GOD**. The wide angle means that **I** cover everywhere, here and there. You are able to cover any part of **LIFE** that you **UNDERSTAND**. If you **UNDERSTAND** your job, you will cover the job. If you **UNDERSTAND** someone, you will cover that person and it would not be easy to crash with someone that you **UNDERSTAND**. If you **UNDERSTAND GOD** thereby **UNDERSTANDING** this **WISDOM**, you would not strife, you would not hate, you would not be jealous and you would not hate anyone and you would not hate this **WORD**. If you are the **LOVER** of **GOOD** things and you gain access to this **MANUAL**, you will be thanking **GOD**. You would be donating heavily to enable the spread of this **WORD** through out the **WHOLE WORLD**. If you are a **GOOD** person and someone that has asked yourself why the world is filled with evil, and has been preaching to people in an attempt to change people, but yet things have not changed then you would support the **HOLY SPIRIT OF THE FATHER GOD** in this **MANUAL**. You will support this movement by helping in whatever way that you can to **PROMOTE** this Lecture Revelation so that people can change and save themselves and their souls. If you are a church leader, a president, head of state, or any post that you may hold you should stop self promoting and **PROMOTE THE FATHER GOD THE CREATOR OF THE UNIVERSE**. Do not say that it is the Senior Servant HRM King Solomon **ETE** that is talking because it is not. From the time of old, **I** have being **TALKING** through human beings. **I TALK** through you in a different way.

Satan speaks through people. **I TALK** through people, however, is it not a thing of **JOY** and **HAPPINESS** that in this last dispensation, **I** have brought out **THE MANUAL OF HOW TO SPEAK** as **THE MANUAL OF THE WORD** and **THE MANUAL OF LIFE** and many other **MANUALS** for general Life? Is it not a wonderful thing? It is something that every earth dweller should celebrate and thank **ME THE FATHER GOD ALMIGHTY** because it means that **GOD'S** kingdom has **TRULY** established on earth. And now, **I THE PERSONIFIED HOLY SPIRIT OF TRUTH** has also **TRULY** established on earth. **I** know that the whole world would take this **MANUAL** seriously, but if you choose not to then you destroy your **LIFE**, but those who take this on board shall preserve their **SOUL**.

This is the **LIFE PRESERVER**! This is the **LIFE BANK**, the **LIFE SECURITY**, the **LIFE INSURANCE** and the **LIFE GUARANTOR**. Buried in this **MANUAL** and the **MANUAL OF THE WORD** is everything that is **GOOD** and every **GOOD** thing. This is why **THE WISDOM OF GOD** covers everywhere as the wide angle of **ME**. Anyone who has **UNDERSTANDING** and **WISDOM** has no problem again. Since **I** have given you the spirit to **UNDERSTAND** this **WORD** then you would **LINK** up with **MY WISDOM**, as the wide angle of **GOD** and then you would not have problems again.

The president, the governor, the head of state, the teacher, the family head, a father, a mother, a manager, a director, a church leader, mosque leader and religious leader, a spirit, an angel and indeed any creation that would use this **MANUAL** to govern as their guide in all endeavours would not have any query from **ME**. However, outside of this, you must prepare yourself for a wonderful query because you have become a betrayer and wanted soul. On the other hand, if you support this **MANUAL**, you will become **MY SERVANT** and **I** shall bless you and bless your offspring. **I** will continue to **IMPROVE** you and give you the opportunity to take an **EVOLUTION** to a better **LIFE** because you have supported **LIFE**! It is **LIFE HIMSELF** as **THE WORD** that has given **HIMSELF** this **MANUAL**, therefore it is for you to know how you can support **HIM** and use **HIM** to get a better **LIFE**.

CONCLUSION A: **ONE WORLD WITH A PERFECT SUPREME FUTURE**

I would establish the **PERFECT** world through this Lecture Revelation and the **MANUAL OF THE WORD**, and that is **MY** aim and objective. You should go and read the Lecture Revelation about the **SUPREME FUTURE** and then you would know. **I AM** giving this Lecture Revelation because **I** have already given the Lecture Revelation tilted *THE SUPREME FUTURE*. The **PERFECT**

FUTURE would come into existence and materialise through this directive. The **PERFECT FUTURE** is what **I** would establish in the entire world and these two **MANUALS** on **HOW TO SPEAK THE WORD** and **THE MANUAL OF LIFE** with others would manage it.

Presently you are borrowing **LIFE**, as a human being, but you must stop barrowing **LIFE**, (*no more, borrow, borrow!*). If you do not accept this Lecture Revelation and practice it then you are a borrower and **I** will subject you to those who **BELIEVE** and **ACCEPT** this **WORD**. Anyone that believes this **WORD** and puts it into practice would be highly placed in **LIFE** and this **WORD** would make such a person an upper self individual. **I** would place those who refuse to believe and apply this **WORD** under those who **BELIEVE** because they would become a servant and a slave to them. And anyone that practices evil and wickedness is doing something that is outside of this **MANUAL**; therefore, **I** would subdue them to be the least. If you **PROMOTE MY WORD**, **I** will **PROMOTE** you very, very high, but if you **DEMOTE MY WORD**, **I** will **DEMOTE** you very, very low.

Song:
If you **PROMOTE MY WORD**, ***I*** *will* **PROMOTE** *you very high, if you* **PROMOTE MY WORD**, ***I*** *will* **PROMOTE** *you high, high.*

But if you **DEMOTE MY WORD**, ***I*** *will* **DEMOTE** *you very low;* ***I*** *will* **DEMOTE** *you low, low.*

That is what it is. If you **PROMOTE MY WORD**, **I** will **PROMOTE** you very high: high, high, but if you **DEMOTE MY WORD** by staying in your corner and saying things like 'oh who is talking' or even make the slightest negative comment about this Lecture Revelation, **I** would **DEMOTE** you. If you like, bet **ME**! It would be a blessing for all the people that start well by **PROMOTING THE TRUTH** which is **THE SUPREME FUTURE, THE LIFE ETERNAL**.

Some people say things such as, 'why does **GOD** not come down, why does **GOD** not change the world, why does **GOD** not destroy the world and so on and so forth'. You want **ME** to destroy the **WORLD**? Is that why people are doing all sorts of evil things so that **I THE FATHER GOD** will be annoyed and destroy the world? You must be very stupid, because when you invest time to construct something and an evil person comes and says that, that thing is not **GOOD** then you destroy it and go back and start again ha? Do you think that **I AM** stupid? **I AM** not destroying the world again, because the world would continue to **LIVE** for eternity, but **I** would destroy you, the evil person. **I** would destroy all evil things and leave the world that **I** have created for **GOOD** people to **LIVE** in it. From this Lecture Revelation, **I** will know that **I** have **GOOD** people, those who are born through **LOVE**, through **PEACE**, through **JOY** and **HAPPINESS** and are born through this **WORD**. Even as **I AM TALKING** now, there are people who will give birth to this **WORD**. As **I AM TALKING** now, if you read or here this **MANUAL** and accept and practice and thank **GOD**, when you give birth your child would be this **WORD** and that is how the world would continue to change. When these types of children are born, they would become the flag bearers of the **SUPREME FUTURE** new world.

The people, the tribe, the family of origin or any human being that accepts **MY WORD** for **THE PERFECT NEW WORLD** and accepts this **ORDER** and this **MANUAL** believing **THE WORD OF GOD, THE FATHER'S TALK**, that it is **POSITIVE** and **THE TRUTH**, would become a flag bearer as one of **MY** many **SELVES** that would incarnate into this world.

This means that **I** would **PERSONALLY** be born through you as one of **THE WORD** that would become a child that would come into your home to change the family. And you will see that from there the whole world would gradually change for **GOOD**. And since **I AM ADA-USUNG (THE LEADER)** of everything and the **CREATOR OF ALL THINGS**, **I** have a way to seize all negativisms on earth. If you do anything to **PROMOTE** evil, you and it will die. If you do anything to **PROMOTE** your evil aims and objectives by creating weapons, through science or any other means that creates deadly poisons and other things that would destroy the world, you are dead and finished. And when you die as you will definitely die, then you shall never be born again, rather **I** will give the opportunity to all **GOD SELVES** to multiply into millions and replant them and **I** will guide them as the **GOOD** spirits that would change the world. And for those of you who voluntary choose to be wicked by standing with Satan and evil to destroy the world, then you have destroyed your soul and you shall never be born again and your total offspring of evil and wickedness is dead. All of your blood line is dead. Everyone should wait and see because **I** have way to eradicate all evil in this world, no matter who you are and how big or influential that you may be or even the amount of money that you have, so far as you are evil, you have no **LIFE** here, there and everywhere. And as you do not have **LIFE** and you cannot bribe **ME THE FATHER GOD THE CREATOR OF THE UNIVERSE, THE LIFE SPEAKING** and **KICKING** with your money or whatever power that you think that you have, then when you finish, you finish forever and **I** meant it. The conclusion for **THE ONE WORLD OF THE SUPREME PERFECT FUTURE** is via this directive. If you adhere to this directive then prepare yourself for enjoyment with your **ME THE FATHER GOD** for eternity. You will enjoy in the present, in the future and you will go and come back and enjoy and it would go on and on and on without an end, so far as you sign on with **ME** through these **MANUALS OF GENERAL LIFE**. From hence forth you are matching **FORWARD** to **THE SUPREME FUTURE OF GOD**.

CONCLUSION B: **WE ARE ONE BRETHREN**

What does **ONE BRETHREN** mean? It means **BROTHERHOOD**. When **I TALK** about **BROTHERHOOD** people argue in their narrow minds, but **I** do not mean the brotherhood of Satan, that Satan has established called white brotherhood, black brotherhood and so forth. This is the cunning of Satan. Just like Satan led people to promote sex as love. They call sexuality love so that anytime that you talk about love it is pertaining to sexuality. If a woman says to a man,

'I love you', she is directly thinking about fornication. If a man says to a woman 'I love you', he is directly thinking about sex, but that is the satanic plan. Satan hijacks the **POSITIVE WORD** and uses it negatively. Today, **I** have corrected Satan's craftiness of trying to change **LOVE** to mean fornication, *just like Satan used her cunning manner to establish on earth, a day of celebration on the day that serpent through Eve deceived Adam and they ate the forbidden fruit called Valentine day and it is the same day that Queen Sheba celebrated sexuality in the temple of sexuality activities*. And this is why anytime that you hear **THE WORD LOVE**, do not think about fornication because fornication does not mean **LOVE**, it means rubbing or sex in your language or intimacy intercourse, natural body interaction or oneself relation. It means flirting and doing nonsense with your body. If you do it correctly with a partner with an actual sense of belonging together with likeness then that means, you have united yourself with that person and whatever comes out from there as a result, the two of you should take it, but that is not **LOVE**. If you call that **LOVE** then what will, you call **ME THE FATHER GOD THE CREATOR OF THE UNIVERSE**. What will you call this **WORD**, what do you call this **INSPIRATION** and what will you call the **HOLY SPIRIT**? Do you not see the mind of Satan? From today through these **MANUALS OF GENERAL LIFE**, the whole world should correct their mind. Do not say to someone 'I love you' when you hate that person. Do you not notice that when you tell someone that 'I love you too much and three much', you go and fight and quarrel, because the love that you are talking about is pertaining to sex, rubbing, fornication exchanging blood and not the actual **LOVE**. **LOVE** means tolerance, **LOVE** means equality, **LOVE** means endurance and that means that wherever that person is you cannot count sin for that person rather you will be **LOVING** that person to do **GOOD** and **THINK WELL** and **SPEAK WELL** of that person. **LOVE** is an entity that shares things equally therefore, those that **LOVE** should **LOVE** properly. Not when you tell someone that you love that person because of wanting to have sex with them or they do that to you. That is the work of Satan because the work of love in Satan's queendom means sex and to have union with someone. The **LOVE OF GOD** in **GOD'S** kingdom means oneness, equality, and the sharer of **GOOD** things. It means sharing every **GOOD** thing together with someone that you **LOVE**. That is the correction that **I** have made today and it stands corrected forever.

People say that we are brotherhood but what type of brotherhood are you? Are you a brotherhood of evil practice such as belonging to secret societies such as freemasons, or brotherhood of performing rituals or brotherhood of witchcraft or what type of brotherhood do you mean? No evil group can be brotherhood of any negativism. **I** have seized it and **I** will sue anyone that claims to be a brotherhood of any type of negative practice. **I** have corrected every mind from the moment that you read this Lecture Revelation. All the people that call themselves brotherhood of any negativism are wanted people and you shall see what their **LIFE** would become, because they will all destroy themselves due to their negative tendencies. You cannot be a **BROTHERHOOD** as a 'part'. You can only be **BROTHERHOOD** as a whole.

BROTHERHOOD means that **GOD THE FATHER THE CREATOR OF THE UNIVERSE** with all his creation spiritually, in the soul and physically form **BROTHERHOOD**. However, since **BROTHERHOOD** is established with mixtures of everything, **I** have now come to synchronize, sanitize and divine it with **THE HOLY SPIRIT** as, **GOD'S DIVINE SELF**. It is for this reason that **I** have brought **BROTHERHOOD OF THE CROSS** and **STAR**. The **CROSS** in **BROTHERHOOD** is the narrow channel of **LOVE** that you must overcome so that if you come from the general **BROTHERHOOD** to the elected **BROTHERHOOD** of the **STAR** then you are a **TRUTHFUL BROTHERHOOD**. Through this **MANUAL OF LIFE** and the **MANUAL OF HOW TO SPEAK THE WORD**, **I** want to see that as many people as can, cross from **BROTHERHOOD** of generality of everything created to **BROTHERHOOD** of **PERFECTION** of **LOVE**, but you cannot claim not to be **BROTHERHOOD**, because by nature everybody is **BROTHERHOOD**. However, for you to sign up to the **PERFECT BROTHERHOOD** of the new world as **THE SUPREME FUTURE**, you have to **LOVE ONE ANOTHER**. You can be wherever you are and practice **BROTHERHOOD** because **BROTHERHOOD** is not pertaining to a church, or a congregation that gathers in a particular place. **BROTHERHOOD** means all creation, seen and unseen including **ME THE SUPREME BEING, THE FATHER GOD, THE CREATOR OF THE UNIVERSE**. This means that everything is **BROTHERHOOD**, but are we **ONE** in **LOVE**, in **NATURE**, in **PEACE**, in **UNDERSTANDING** and **WISDOM**? If we are all **ONE** in **POSITIVISM** then all is well. If this be the case then we are all **BRETHREN** and that is **BROTHERHOOD**. If we are **BRETHREN** then we must **LOVE**, because if you hate anyone and think any evil about anyone then you are thinking that about yourself and that is why you will surely reap what you sow. Everybody came from **ONE GOD THE FATHER ADAM, THE FIRST SPOKEN WORD MANIFEST** and **I THE FATHER GOD THE CREATOR OF THE UNIVERSE** is the source and the destination and that is the reason why you must **LOVE ONE ANOTHER**. It is the **COMPULSORY TASK** that everyone must do this and follow this **MANUAL**.

CONCLUSION C: **ONE PARENT, GOD ALMIGHTY**

ONE PARENT, GOD ALMIGHTY is **BROTHERHOOD. THE SUPREME PARENT** is **ME THE FATHER GOD.** By your word, you shall be condemned and by your word, you shall be justified. **I THE FATHER GOD ALMIGHTY, I AM THE SUPREME WORD** and this **MANUAL OF LIFE** and **THE MANUAL OF HOW TO SPEAK THE WORD** is the **REMEDY** for every situation. It is the directive for governing the new world of **THE SUPREME FUTURE**. Also, you must **INSTINCTIVELY UNDERSTAND** without anyone having to beg and plead with you. You must voluntarily **UNDERSTAND** with **BELIEVE** if you are **TRUTHFUL** to your spirit soul in your heart, because if you read and listen with humility, you would know that this is **THE WORD SPOKEN** direct by **ME THE FATHER GOD** and not the word by a human being. With this **UNDERSTANDING**, you would willingly adopt the said **MANUALS** for your spirit, your soul and your physical **LIFE** now and in the **FUTURE** so that for generations of generations you shall to be a part of **THE FATHER GOD'S SUPREME FUTURE**. However, if you do not do this then you have taken a voluntary evolution to exclude yourself from **ME** and good luck to your soul; because you are on your own and whatever happens to your soul do not blame **GOD** because your blood will be upon you.

I revealed **MYSELF** in **HOW TO SPEAK THE WORD** and **I AM** again revealing **MYSELF** in **HOW TO LIVE LIFE** titled **THE MANUAL OF LIFE**. With these two Lecture Revelations and the rest of the **MANUALS** and all the **FATHER'S TALK** (**GOD PRESENT**) Lecture Revelations, all is well with the entire world now and forever, more, *Amien*.

In the name of Our Lord Jesus the Christ, In the blood of Our Lord Jesus the Christ, Now and forever, more, *Amien*.

ENYE ODUDU ABASI ME, OOO ZIM ZIM ASASU, POSITIVE, POSITIVE, POSITIVE!

THANK YOU FATHER

Prayer of thanks by: **HRM Queen Disem**

Let thanks and praises be given to **THE FATHER** in the name of Our Lord Jesus Christ.
Let thanks and praises be given to **THE FATHER** in the blood of Our Lord Jesus Christ.
Let thanks and praises be given to **THE HOLY SPIRIT** of **TRUTH, LEADER OLUMBA OLUMBA OBU** now and forever, more, *Amien*.
HOLY, HOLY FATHER.

Thank **YOU FATHER** for this day of **CREATION**, Thank **YOU FATHER** for giving us this **MANUAL** for all creation to use because as **YOU** have said anyone that drives a car must know how to drive a car so that one would not harm themselves and harm others and so it must be with **LIVING LIFE**. Thank **YOU FATHER** for bringing the **MANUAL** of **LIFE** so that we will **LIVE** a **LIFE** that is useful to our selves and others and that would bring **GLORY** to **THEE** for eternity and all will be well with all creation even now and forever, more, *Amien*.

Let thanks and praises be given to **THE FATHER** in the name of Our Lord Jesus Christ.
Let thanks and praises be given to **THE FATHER** in the blood of Our Lord Jesus Christ.
Let thanks and praises be given to **THE CREATOR OF THE UNIVERSE**, **THE LIFE FORCE** through **WHOM** we can all have **LIFE** through this **MANUAL** now and forever, more, *Amien*.

THANK YOU FATHER
=========

CHAPTER THREE

INVESTMENT WITH THE FATHER GOD

FATHER'S TALK
(GOD PRESENT)

Date: BA/AO/OG (The twenty first day of the tenth month of **THE FATHER** 'year' two thousand and seven)

In the Name of Our Lord Jesus Christ, In the Blood of Our Lord Jesus Christ, Now and forever more, *Amien*.

INVESTMENT WITH THE FATHER GOD

Blessed are those who thirst and hunger because of righteousness as they shall be filled. They shall be in abundance. Blessed are the poor saint and those who lack because of following the way of **THE GOOD GOD** and for being righteous, and as a result they have **GOD** in their minds so they decide to stay as they are and as **THE FATHER GOD** has kept them. Blessed are these because **I** shall bountifully provide for them and they shall inherit the kingdom of **GOD**.

Today is the day that **I** have decided to honour **MY** promise made on the BA/AO/OG (twenty first day of the tenth month the year two thousand and seven) that **I** will give a Lecture Revelation titled **INVESTMENT WITH THE FATHER GOD**. Many generations before the creation of human beings, **I** was doing business with other creations. These were animals, birds' fishes, and other living creatures and living organisms, but **I** did not gain from them. For generations upon generations, **I** have not had any gain. What kind of business is that when you do not gain? **I AM** a **TYPICAL BUSINESS FATHER GOD**, a **BUSINESS SUPER SPIRITUAL NATURAL**; therefore **I** must gain from **MY BUSINESS**. Today, **I AM** going to reveal the meaning of **BUSINESS**, the proper **BUSINESS** when one talks about **BUSINESS** which is not about committing crimes, creating havoc, committing sin and being unrighteous. **BUSINESS** means **GOD**, because **I AM** busy twenty four hours in creation, in blessing, in improvement, in encouragement and progression and that is **BUSINESS**. **BUSINESS** means development, improvement and evolution. The people of this world do not know the meaning of **BUSINESS**, but today because of this Lecture Revelation titled **INVESTMENT WITH GOD, I AM** now revealing what the **WORD 'BUSINESS'** means. The actual word **B-U-S-I-N-E-S-S** means **BE USEFUL SINCERE INTER NATURE ESSENCE SELF SACRIFICE**. And in the spiritual language, the above word **BUSINESS** is **ARISANTICE**. **ARISANTICE** means one thing that links to others and becomes one in total. In the real sense whatever that you do should be beneficial to others which is tantamount to **LOVE** for all creation. In the English language, the word **BUSINESS** is as denoted above, but in other languages the meaning remains the same, but may differ in spelling and breakdown of its subsequent translation.

I AM THE SPOKEN WORD; I AM THE ONLY ONE that engineers **WORD** to know the meaning of any language, any sentence and open **WORD** on earth. You speak the **WORD**, but you do not know that **I** can decode all the **WORDS** that came out of your mouth. The **WORD** '**BUSINESS**' is attached to today's revelation, **INVESTMENT WITH GOD'S BUSINESS** but first, **I** have to give the introduction for this Lecture Revelation.

INTRODUCTION

The Lecture Revelation of today comes as an enhancement and **NONE STOP PERMANENT BLESSING** continuity as a promise of **GOD** to all **FAITHFUL** human **GODS** on earth. **I** mean all positive children of **GOD** as the children of Adam that have reincarnated and resurrected which means they are the children of repentance, the children that believe that **CHRIST** has died and used His precious blood to wipe away their sins. As a result, they are waiting to **PROMOTE GOD**, to **LOVE GOD** and **INHERIT THE KINGDOM OF GOD** for eternity. **I AM** giving this Lecture Revelation for these sets of human beings. This Lecture Revelation is for those who believe in **ME THE FATHER GOD** as the children of Abraham and that engulfs every type of human being including, the human **GOD**, human fish, human animal and human bird and any other type of developed human being on earth. However, the point of correction that **I** want to bring before the actual Lecture Revelation is that human beings should **LOVE** themselves because they all came out of one source. The **SOURCE** and the **DESTINATION** is only one. The Father of all physical human beings is Adam and that is why Abraham is the father of all nations. Abraham is the representative father on earth as the house and the soul of Adam in the human natural form. Abraham is the promise child of **GOD** that **GOD** promised to bring to represent **HIM**. And that is why he offered Isaac as a sacrifice so that when **I** come to this earth as Our Lord Jesus Christ, **I** will successfully die and use **MY** blood and water to wash away man's sins and that is the meaning of children of **GOD**.

From the moment that you hear this Lecture Revelation, you must stop causing segregation on earth between Ishmael and Isaac. Abraham is the father on earth and through him, **I** have made all the nations full, because all children of **GOD** on earth are children of Abraham likewise the children of Adam, therefore there should be no segregation, no jealousy and strife or division of any kind. **LOVE** is the answer for all humankind on earth. There is no Black or White or any colour of people. All are one in **ME THE FATHER GOD**. As every human being has blood and water and the word living in them, then that means that, the **TRINITY GOD**, **THE FATHER SON** and **HOLY SPIRIT** representing the spirit, the soul and the physical body are in them. This means that you are a complete human being and the colour of your skin does not matter, because you may be Solid skin person or Soft skin person (Black or White) in this generation, but in another time, you may be born a different colour from your previous colour. And if you hate 'Black' people, when you are born another time as a Black person, a Black person would hate you. And if you hate a 'White' person, when you are born as a White person, a White person would hate you. And if you are a man that hates women, when you are born as a woman, a woman would hate you and vice versa and that is why you should **LOVE** one another and do not hate anything unless it is evil, because **LOVE** is the **FOCAL** and **CENTRAL POINT** of contention in the whole universe.

The children of Abraham were Ishmael and Isaac. They were of course brothers with the same father and that is **BROTHERHOOD** therefore, **I** have established the kingdom of **GOD**. And anyone who does not embrace the teachings of **THE HOLY SPIRIT** in Brotherhood of the Cross and Star cannot claim to be the decedents of the children of Abraham. However not all are children of Abraham. It is only those who believe that they should **LOVE** and unite together in the entire world that can claim to be in Brotherhood of the Cross and Star in practical terms and not theory and that is **MY BUSINESS**. This is the **BUSINESS** that **I AM** establishing now which is to unite the whole world together. It is not a matter of Christianity or Islam or indeed any other religion or non religion. Everybody is Brotherhood and that is what **CHRIST** died for so that the whole world would unite together in **LOVE**. **THE FATHER GOD** is **LOVE** as one **SPIRIT**, one **SOUL** and one **WORD** and that is why everybody speaks the **WORD** and for that reason you can interpret, every language into one language. 'IMA' means **LOVE** in the Ibibio or Efik language and that is the same as **LOVE** in the English language. You can put what you call a White man's blood that matches in terms of type of blood into what you call a Black man's system and he would survive and vice-versa, as such what is the difference? The only difference is jealousy which is evil. Abraham has **ONE GOD** and that **GOD** is **ME THE FATHER GOD ALMIGHTY** the one that inspired his spirit and life and made him the Father of all nations and that is why **I** have put all Muslims, Christians and all other religions together in one fold called Brotherhood of the Cross and Star. The Cross means that you must **LOVE** your brother. A Christian must copy the life style of **CHRIST** by **LOVING** Muslims and other religions on earth. Every Christian must embrace all religions, because they are the Father and Mother of all religions. Since **CHRIST** has died to unite the whole world, any **CHRISTIAN** who does not accept to suffer and carry the Cross by embracing every human being and every creation will not have anything to do with **CHRIST**. And that is why **I** say that if you do not carry your **CROSS** and follow after **ME**, then you are not worthy of **ME**. And equally, any Muslim who does not **LOVE** Christians is a condemned soul because Abraham is the Father of both. That is why **I** have now established the kingdom of **GOD** as Brotherhood meaning the children of the same parents. Cross means that you are to carry one another's burden and Star means that after we have successfully **LOVED** ourselves, there would be no more killing, no more fighting, no more problems and that happiness and successful unity is called Star hence the name, **BROTHERHOOD OF THE CROSS AND STAR**.

You can be Brotherhood, but that does not mean that you are doing well unless you **LOVE ONE ANOTHER** and when you achieve that then **I** will upgrade you from Cross to **STAR** and that is **MY BUSINESS**. I will elevate any soul who is able to do this irrespective of them being a man, a woman or Black or White or Christian or Muslim and any other religion. **I** will then choose you to be one of the people that would lead the whole nation. And that is the introduction of this Lecture Revelation.

A: **HOW TO DO BUSINESS WITH ME THE FATHER GOD**

Everyone should ask himself or herself this question in that since **THE FATHER GOD** is the creator of heaven and earth who should we copy, and what type of character should we portray so that we would resemble **THE FATHER GOD** as our creator? We are to recognize **GOD** by being **HONEST, FAITHFUL** and **LOVE ONE ANOTHER**. First, you must know that **GOD** is your **FATHER**. You cannot do **BUSINESS** with someone that you do not know and **UNDERSTAND** his or her language. Since **I** have revealed and given **THE MANUAL OF THE SPOKEN WORD** which is **THE INTRODUCTION OF INVESTMENT WITH GOD**, now it is the real **BUSINESS. INVESTMENT WITH GOD** is to **BELIEVE** that your **CREATOR** is in **EXISTENCE**. Some people say that **THE FATHER GOD** does not **EXIST**. That makes those people liars, because you are not honest in your conscience. If you think that there is no **FATHER GOD** then you must prove it. If you are a scientist or whatever that you think that you are then prove to **ME** how you have decided that there is nothing like **ME THE FATHER GOD** and nothing like **YOUR THE CREATOR** and that everything just came out in the blue moon and remained like that. Who has the **BLUE PRINT** of all **CREATION**? **I AM THE FATHER GOD THE CREATOR OF THE UNIVERSE. THE CREATOR** in the first place is **THE SPOKEN WORD**. It is **THE SPOKEN WORD** in the heaven and on earth physically and that is the **ADMINISTRATOR** as **THE ALL AND ALL**. Show **ME** anything that anyone does without **THE WORD** and since you manipulate **THE WORD** to do what you want to do then, it is either you are successful in your way or you are not. However, **I THE FATHER GOD THE CREATOR OF THE UNIVERSE** has revealed that every creation seen and unseen and all human beings should humble themselves and believe that whoever that you may be, you have a **CREATOR** and a **SPONSOR** who is the **EFFECT** before you came to be. The **CAUSE** of creating you, the

CAUSE of you becoming a living thing and the **CAUSE** of everything is **I THE FATHER GOD THE CREATOR OF THE UNIVERSE**. And that is how you manifested on earth as a house of **THE SPOKEN WORD**. For this reason, when you know this and have the **MANUAL OF THE SPOKEN WORD**, then you will know how to **SPEAK THE WORD** and that is how **MY BUSINESS** with you starts.

You do **BUSINESS** with **ME THE FATHER GOD** by first of all **BELIEVING** in **ME** and after that, you must acknowledge **MY** presence as the **EXISTENCE** and the **TOTALITY** of **TOTALITIES** in every creation. Once you know all these, then that would be the initial premise for signing on to do **BUSINESS** with **ME THE FATHER GOD, YOUR ORIGINAL CREATOR**.

B: **FAITH WITH THE FATHER GOD**

First, you must have **FAITH** with **ME THE FATHER GOD ALMIGHTY**. **FAITH** is the key holder as **THE BUSINESS PLAN**. Out of **LOVE**, **FAITH** and **HOPE, FAITH is THE BUSINESS PLAN**. Before you do something with someone, you need to establish **BELIEVING** through the information that you have received via an advert or news or from any other source and when you **BELIEVE** in the initial introduction of that product and the story then you will yield **FAITH**. After that, you can promote the product or that **BUSINESS** if by so doing you will make more money. From this, you will then apply to become an agent, but before you become an agent, you will test the product for yourself and once you **BELIEVE** and have **FAITH**, then you have passed the first examination. And that is why **LOVE** is the answer because you must **LOVE ME, THE FATHER GOD** with all your strength and your entire mind and then you will have **UNDERSTANDING** through which you will have **FAITH** and that would create the awareness that **I THE FATHER AM** the only **PHENOMENON** to be involved with for **BUSINESS**. And with this you would, practice the five major attributes of **MY-SELF** called the **FIVE BLESSED STARS** and that is **MERCY, LOVE RIGHTEOUSNESS, KINDNESS** and **PEACE**. When you practice these five major stars then you are standing on a rock that will never fail you. Through that inspiration, **I THE FATHER GOD** will also have **TRUST** in you, because you have established **FAITH** in **ME** by believing that **I AM** the rock as the foundation stone. **FAITH** is the rock as such **FAITH** is the key holder where all others would hang without failure. The first requirement in **BUSINESS** with **ME THE FATHER GOD** is **BELIEVE** and **FAITH**. Since you have established **BELIEVE** and **FAITH** and **HOPE** with

ME THE FATHER GOD, it means that you have now signed on to promote the **PRODUCTS** of **GOD**. What are the **PRODUCTS** of **GOD**? What is the **BUSINESS** of **GOD** that you have to **PROMOTE**? There are many, but you must first **PROMOTE** the spiritual **PRODUCTS**. And they are **LOVE**, having **MERCY**, being **PEACEFUL**, being **PATIENT**, being **KIND** and being **RIGHTEOUS**. All these components prove that you are a person of **GOD** with integrity and respect. A spiritual person for whom, left to you, there would be **PEACE** reigning everywhere in the world. You should not be someone that when people see you they hide because they believe that you are going to kill, harass or make their life difficult in one way or the other. These are types of people that display pomposity, arrogance, aggression and are easily angered and if such people are in positions as presidents, prime ministers, church leaders, other types of heads of countries, institutions or groups, communities and families, they should be gotten rid off. These are evil ills that make you as an individual or head of anything to manifest the will of Satan if you attach yourself to or portray such characters.

If you have **LOVE** and are **VERY PATIENT, SIMPLE** and **EASILY ENTREATED**, then you represent **GOD** in your manner and in your attributes, because a child must represent his **FATHER**. A child must resemble his parents. If you represent **GOD** and resemble **GOD** and have the character of **GOD**, that is a **GOOD** thing because that is what **I** want. If you have **LOVE, PATIENCE, HUMILITY, THINK WELL, SPEAK WELL** and **DO WELL** and are **KIND** to people, that will show that, you are ready to **PROMOTE MY BUSINESS**. That would be the will, the vow, the agreement and the promise that you have with **ME** and in turn, **I** will use you to manifest **MY GLORY**. From this premise, **MY BUSINESS** with you has started and the next stage is an appreciative heart.

C: **APPRECIATIVE HEART**

Through **FAITH**, Abraham was willing to sacrifice Isaac to **GOD**. If you **LOVE** someone, you will sacrifice everything about you for that person. **LOVE** is **FAITH** and **SELF SURRENDER** to the object of your **LOVE**. When a woman **LOVES** a man, she subjects herself to that man and when a man **LOVES** a woman, he **LOVES** that woman therefore **LOVE** means **SUBJECTION** and **SUBJECTION** means **LOVE**. And that is a characteristic of **APPRECIATION. SELF SURRENDER, SELF AWARENESS** and **HUMILITY** mean that you **APPRECIATE ME THE FATHER GOD** through your conduct and in your way of life. If you **LOVE ME THE FATHER GOD** with all your strength, all your might and your entire mind and have

FAITH in **ME**, then everything that **I** keeps in your possession in-turn belongs to **ME**. You should use all that you have to **APPRECIATE ME THE FATHER GOD** and **INVEST** in **ME**. When you **INVEST** under this capacity, then you are doing **BUSINESS** with **ME THE FATHER GOD**. The next stage in this process is to be **TRUTHFUL**.

D: **BEING TRUTHFUL**

Before showing **APPRECIATION** to **ME THE FATHER GOD** that **I** will accept, you must be **TRUTHFUL**. You cannot be **TRUTHFUL** or **FAITHFUL** to someone when you hide somewhere and do something, then present another face to the person. And that is why you must **THINK WELL, SPEAK WELL, SEE WELL** and **HEAR WELL** before you can **DO WELL**. You must be **TRUTHFUL** to someone that you **LOVE** and want to show **APPRECIATION** to. Due to the stage that you are, you may not be able to be a hundred percent **TRUTHFUL**, but if you are up to seventy percent then **I THE FATHER GOD** will balance the rest for you, but if it is lower that fifty percent then **I** cannot sign on with you completely, but you must start to be faithful to **ME**, let say by thirty percent, then that will make **MY** spirit to start coming nearer to you.

You say that you are **TRUTHFUL** to **GOD**, but anytime that you come across a little temptation; you go and look for soothsayers, native doctors or a juju man and others that claim to be able to help you so you fall down at their feet, but you do not know if they believe in **ME THE FATHER GOD**. You can only go to someone that you have tested their spirit to know if truly they really worship **ME THE FATHER GOD**. When you go to someone to pray for you or go to someone to do any spiritual thing for you, **I** ask you, do you know the energy that the person uses? If that person belongs to a secret society or they are an arm robber or a killer or are involved in any negative endeavour and you go to that person to give you money then he or she will go and kill people to give you that money, because you want help from that person. Indirectly, you are the one that killed, because he or she killed to bring money for you. As soon as you go to get help from that person, you are the client and therefore, the sponsor that enables that person to do what they are doing. And that is why any child of **GOD** does not attach to people without being sure of what that person stands for.

You should attach yourself to **ME THE FATHER GOD** in someone not to the person per se. However, before you attach to someone, you should be sure that **I THE FATHER GOD** resides in that person and then you attach to **ME THE FATHER GOD** through him or her. Other than that, you cannot be sure of what you have attached to and if you attach to someone without being sure that the person hass attached themselves to **GOD** then you are automatically, attached to whatever that person has attached himself or herself to, and that is when you are not **TRUTHFUL**. You may think that you are **TRUTHFUL**, but because you attach yourself to someone who is an idol worshiper, a witch or wizard or is involved in any other evil practice, then automatically, you are feeding from evil and if any thing happens to you, you will blame **GOD** and ask 'why is my life is like this, and why is my life is like that and why should **I** have bad dreams' but you do not know that you have attached your soul to someone that is evil and what you are experiencing is the outcome of that attachment. Any day that you speak to an evil person or accompany an evil person, that night, you will see a sign of evil and immediately, you will feel the impact of evil. It is the same thing in the opposite way that happens when evil people come closer to children of **GOD**; they feel a **LIGHT** as though something is trying to penetrate into them to kill the evil because of the **LIGHT** of a child of **GOD**. And that is why you must be **TRUTHFUL** to **GOD** in everything that you are doing in your heart and be sure of what you are doing by not going left and right. You should centralise your mind. Once you can do this then **I THE FATHER GOD** can establish a **CERTIFICATE OF INCORPORATION** with you.

In the spirit of **TRUTH, I** will give you a '**CERTIFICATE OF INCORPORATION**' to do **BUSINESS** with **ME THE FATHER GOD** because you are honest to your soul and that is the meaning of cross. You will see temptation, because Satan would tempt you and that would sanctify you to **GOD**. All the things that you pass through in your life are to enable you to get that certificate that would prove that you are okay in that you are **TRUTHFUL** to **GOD**. A wife and a husband must go through the period of trails with each other and when they conquer, they become a proper wife and husband. It is not a matter of going to court or a church to marry, doing eye service to show people that this is my husband or wife. That is not the actual meaning of being married. You must pass the test of marriage. The period of honey-mooning will pass and temptation and trails must surely come. Misunderstanding will come, but when two of you pass that stage and start to understand yourselves and are **FAITHFUL** and **TRUTHFUL** to each other, then the **STAR** has come and that is the time that you can believe that you are actually husband and wife. The same thing applies to every relationship as parents and their children, brothers and sisters, friends, colleagues and all other types of relationships must undergo the period of trials and when you pass, then you can be sure of that relationship. At a more macro level within a country, you must undergo such a trail. When you stand for election to become a prime minister or as a president or MP or governor or chairperson of any local government or any other post that requires a service and a vote from people, do you pass the test by fulfilling the promises that you made to people in order to get their vote? Are you able to look after people so that they will feel that you have solved their problems? Are you making any difference from those who came before you? When you pass the test of necessity and the test of **'EVERY OTHER PEOPLES CHORUS'** then that is when you will be a really a different person and that is when you will be happy. You say that you **LOVE THE FATHER GOD** and that **THE FATHER GOD** should **PROMOTE** you and do **BUSINESS** with you. You want **THE FATHER GOD** to elevate you to rule and be in-charge of your family, so that people would know you as a prominent person. And you want **THE FATHER GOD** to talk through you, but do you know that there is a test for all these things? When different spirits come to test you in various forms through your wife, your husband, your child, your friend or fellow brother, or sister in spirit soul and physically you must pass the test. **I** would not leave you comfortless, as **I** will be behind, watching you from the back to monitor the front so as to protect you so that no harm would befall you, because you are doing **BUSINESS** with **GOD**. Any temptation that comes to you is a test because nothing will happen to you, but you must be strong and when you conquer, **I** will give you a **CERTIFICATE OF INCORPORATION** and that is the meaning of **AMFAR-ONE BROSISCO**. **MY FATHER** and **I ARE ONE, BROTHERS AND SISTERS INCORPORATED WITH GOD. AMFAR-ONE BROSISCO** is a spiritual language which means **TRUE UNITY** with **CHRIST** and that is the meaning of **TRUE BROTHERHOOD**. If you do not believe and understand **AMFAR-ONE-BROSISCO** then you should forget about it because you are not a **TRUE BROTHERHOOD**. You say that you are a Christian, you are Muslim, you are a Buddhist, or you are member of any other religion or organization, but that does not really matter because you must register yourself with **THE FATHER'S BUSINESS** and be come one with **ME THE FATHER GOD** as **AMFAR-ONE**. **AMFAR-ONE** is, **I** and **MY FATHER** are one and **BROSISCO** is brothers and sisters incorporated in **CHRIST** and that is when you must not **THINK** any evil, **SPEAK** any evil or **DO** any evil of any kind to anyone or even yourself and that is when you are now signed on with **ME, THE FATHER GOD THE CREATOR OF THE UNIVERSE**. This is when **I** will certify you with the **CERTIFICATE OF INCORPORATION OF LOVE** and that is when you are in **BUSINESS** with **GOD**. Once **I** have certified you, then **I** will give you the **POWER** of conquering and that is when the sign of **MY HOLY SPIRIT** will start to manifest through you. **THE** way you **SPEAK** is **THE FATHER'S TALK**, when you walk, it is **THE FATHER** that is walking, and when you **LOOK**, it is **THE FATHER** that is **LOOKING**. This means that **I** have established **MY** office in you as the **TRINITY GOD**. Your **BLOOD** is **THE FATHER GOD**, your **BODY** is **THE FATHER GOD** and your **WORD** is **THE FATHER GOD**. And that means that spirit, soul, and physical presence of you is **THE FATHER GOD**. Anybody that sees you and talks to you and touches you are doing so to **THE FATHER GOD** and that means that they will see **GOD** in you, they will touch **GOD** in you and they will hear **GOD** in you, because you are now **INCORPORATED** together with **ME THE FATHER GOD** and that is the beginning of **OUR BUSINESS** which would move us to the next stage which is **HABITATION** of **LOVE**,

PEACE, MERCY, RIGHTEOUSNESS and **KINDNESS**.

D: HABITATION OF LOVE, PEACE MERCY, RIGHTEOUSNESS AND KINDNESS

When you reach this stage of being **TRUTHFUL** then, you have become the house of **THE FATHER GOD** and the **HABITATION** of **GOD'S GLORY** and **MY POSITIVE SPIRIT** will come and live in you and shine as a **STAR**. If you have **LOVE, PEACE, MERCY, RIGHTEOUSNESS** and **KINDNESS** then you will become the brightness **STAR**. People would not be able to do any evil thing to you again in this world because you have conquered the world and conquered all negativism which means you are everywhere, here and there with **ME THE FATHER GOD**. You are there with **ME THE FATHER GOD** and you here with **ME THE FATHER GOD**. You will become rich indeed very, very rich and anyone that does any

BUSINESS with you now is doing it indirectly with **ME THE FATHER GOD**. At this juncture, you have become a **STAR** and that means that you are no longer of yourself, because these five stars are manipulating you and you will become a **POSITIVE, POSITIVE, POSITIVE** mysterious person. You no longer exist; it is **ME THE FATHER GOD** that exists in you. And that is what it is under that capacity. From this basis, you become one with **ME THE FATHER GOD THE CREATOR OF THE UNIVERSE**.

E: **BECOMING ONE WITH ME THE FATHER GOD**

 At this stage, you have become **THE FATHER GOD'S** physical representative. Your **THOUGHT** is **THE FATHER'S THOUGHT** and your **WORD** is **THE FATHER'S WORD** and you have become **FATHER'S PRESENT**. You are not **THE FATHER** but you have become **GOD PRESENT**. And this is when the

BUSINESS of **you** and **ME** starts and if someone bows down for you, they are not actually bowing down to you but for **ME THE FATHER GOD** and for that reason you will also bow down because you will not sit down and bring your head for someone to worship you. The way you bow down for **ME THE FATHER GOD** is the same way the person will also bow down for **ME THE FATHER GOD** and that makes you **GOD'S PRESENT**, as a **SHRINE** of **GOD**, a **TEMPLE of GOD** and an **ALTAR** of **GOD**. You are the **TABERNACLE** of **GOD** as **ONE** with **THE FATHER GOD**. You have **POSITIVE, POSITIVE,** and **POSITIVE SPIRIT** of **GOD** in you in the spirit, soul and in the physical **TRUTH**. And since **THE POSITIVE SPIRIT** of **MYSELF THE FATHER GOD** has manifested in you, you will start seeing the **BRIGHTNESS SPIRIT** of **GOD**, as the **TEMPLE** of the living **GOD**, because **I THE FATHER GOD** lives in you therefore, everywhere, here and there, you are one with **ME THE FATHER GOD THE CREATOR OF THE UNIVERSE.** Wherever you are, you are with **THE FATHER GOD**. And no evil can touch you, because you are a representative of **GOD THE FATHER** in human form on earth.

F: **THE GLORY OF GOD MANIFEST IN YOU**

It is at this stage that people would start to doubt, because they would say, 'oh but this person used to be a bad person' but they do not realize that you are no longer a bad person rather you are **GOD PRESENT**. They would say that this person used to be a drunkard; this person used to be a fornicator, this person used to do this and that however the person has become the **DWELLING PLACE OF GOD** therefore you must forget about the past. The **GLORY OF GOD** is manifesting through that person as such the way that person speaks would change and even the physical presence of that person would change. His face would change and his attitude would change and he would always talk about **ME THE FATHER GOD** and **I THE FATHER GOD** talks through him/her, because he or she and **I** are **ONE** and that is **THE GLORY OF GOD MANIFESTING**. If you do something with that person, you are no longer dealing with an ordinary human being; you are dealing with **ME THE FATHER GOD**. If you give him one naira or one pound, you are **DIRECTLY INVESTING** with **ME THE FATHER GOD** and you will never loose. He or she is **GOD PRESENT**, therefore anything that you do with him or her, you are doing with **ME THE FATHER GOD** and you would not loose anything. If you knock your head on the ground, you are not knocking your head for the person rather you are doing it for **ME THE FATHER GOD THE CREATOR OF HEAVEN AND EARTH** that lives in that person. If you greet him you not greeting him, rather you are greeting **ME THE FATHER GOD**. If you **LOVE** him, you do not **LOVE** him rather you **LOVE ME THE FATHER GOD**. Anything that you do to him you are doing to **ME THE FATHER GOD**, because that is where **I THE FATHER GOD** lives and **THE GLORY OF GOD MANIFEST'S** through that person. This is when the person would become a different person, but people would say that everybody is equal. Such a person is no longer equal with you; however, he is equal with everybody through **LOVE**, but not equal in capacity. A city is not the same as a village or a family. A community is not the same as a village. A local government is not the same as a community. The state is not the same as the local government and the country is not the same as the state and a continent as Africa is not the same as a country like Nigeria. And the continent is not the same as the world and the world is not the same as the universe and the universe is not the same as **THE FATHER GOD THE CREATOR OF THE UNIVERSE, THE TOTALITY OF TOTALITIES, THE OWNER, THE IN CHARGE,** (**THE A-Z,** and **ZAKROLL**). Since you now know that the stages, the storage room of capacity and the storage memory is different, you must bow, surrender and be in subjection of yourself to a bigger storage. You also know that such a person has changed and the sign of **THE LIVING GOD** and **HIS GLORY** is manifesting in him/her, then you must attach yourself to that positive person and that means that you have attached yourself to **ME THE FATHER GOD**. That person is the **HOUSE** of **GOD**, **ALTAR** of **GOD** and the **TEMPLE** of **GOD** and that is the kind of person that **I THE FATHER GOD** talks through, and therefore this is **THE BUSINESS** of **GOD**. If you **INVEST** with that person, you are **INVESTING** in **BIG WAY** and you are **INVESTING** in **EVERLASTING LIFE**, with **LOVE** and **SECURITY**. If you go closer to that person then your sickness is over. If you talk to that person then all the evil in you would run away.

I have revealed that some people have cockroach, rat, cat, dog, bird and all other types of animals in them because they have taken an evolution from these planets to become human beings. All these forms are compound human beings here on earth from the bush, the water and other places. They are compound human birds, human fishes and human animals, but they are human's beings. And since these forms are in them, they would continue to operate inside them until such a time that **I THE FATHER GOD** grants another evolution for them when they **CHANGE**. If you go closer to those people, you will have a bad dream. In the spirit-soul, all the creeping things and the animals in the air, in the water and the land connect to the human being in which they dwell. If you come from the moon and have been born here, then all the terrestrial bodies from the moon are in you and using you to operate. Similarly, someone who comes from heaven and is born here on earth has the entire heavenly host in them. The same applies to someone from the water and from any other place that you may come from because you are the way for all the spirits souls from that planet of your origin to come on earth and attach themselves to people therefore, you must be careful of who you attach yourself to. And whom you **INVEST** your hope and your **BUSINESS**. However if you attach yourself to a new evolutional and arranged human **GOD** who is the **HOUSE** of **THE FATHER GOD**, the **TEMPLE** of **THE LIVING GOD** where the **GLORY** of **GOD** manifests through by the way he **THINKS** and **SPEAKS** and **DOES** which are **POSITIVE, POSITIVE, POSITIVE** then all will be well with you. If you put these **WORDS** into practice, then you will also become **POSITIVE, POSITIVE** and **POSITIVE** and whomever that attaches themselves to you will find that **I THE FATHER GOD** solves their problems. If such a person speaks to you, all becomes well with you and to just see that person in the dream, then equally all becomes well with you because you cannot see that person in the negative way since that is **GOD PRESENT**. That is a human **GOD** that has become **THE TEMPLE** of **GOD** because **GOD** does not live in a building that man has built rather, **I** live in the **HOUSE** that **I** have built which is a human being. On the same note if you **THINK** evil and **SPEAK** evil and **PRACTISE** evil, then you will invite the evil spirit soul to come and reside in you. And when people come closer to you, they will see evil in you because you have become the **HOUSE** of evil according to what you practice. However if you want **GOD** to reside in you then you must **THINK WELL, SPEAK WELL** and **DO WELL** and practice **LOVE** for **ONE ANOTHER** and have **PEACE** and all other **GOOD** virtues then all the evil will run away from you. Anyone that comes closer to you will receive **PEACE**. Anyone that comes closer to you will receive **JOY**. For instance, you practice **LOVE** because your heart is full with **LOVE**, as such, any one that comes closer to you will only see **LOVE** and as result, they would also have to practise **LOVE**. By the same token, if you have **FAITH**, those who come close to you will also develop **FAITH**. Equally, if you are a **TRUST WORTHY** and a **TRUTHFUL** person, then those who come to you will automatically become **TRUTHFUL** because the spirit of **TRUTH** will envelope them, and they will start to be **TRUTHFUL** and **POWERFUL** as you. If you represent **LIGHT**, then those who come closer to you will become bright, but if you are darkness then those who come to you will develop more darkness and that is exactly what it is. There is no magic in the whole matter.

(G) *EVERLASTING LIFE*

At this stage of **EVERLASTING LIFE**, all other blessings from **GOD** follow you. Negative people do not like or want to help such a person because he or she has become a different person who no longer follows them to fornicate, gossip, hate, go to war, dupe people and practice all manners of evil. As a result, they ignore him/her, and remove him/her from their gang and community, but **I THE FATHER GOD** has raised him/her up and sent heavenly hosts to accompany him/her everywhere that he/she goes. **I** become his/her hand, **I** become his/her ears, **I** become his/her eyes and nose, and **I** become his /her leg and become everything of everything for that person. And you will be able to see when the **SUPREME SPIRIT, THE SPOKEN WORD HIMSELF** becomes a part and parcel of that person because **MY HAND** can reach anywhere, **MY EYES** can see everything and **I AM**

EVERYWHERE to get whatever **I** want. Such a person has nothing to loose and that is why it is said that one with **THE FATHER** is majority. For this reason, if you help a servant of **GOD** then you help your soul. If you deny a servant of **GOD** something then you deny your soul and if you deprive him/her something then you deprive yourself something. If you barrier a servant of **GOD**, you barrier yourself in something and if you hindrance a servant of **GOD**, you hindrance yourself in something. However if you **LOVE** a servant of **GOD** as **HOUSE** of **GOD**, then you **LOVE** yourself. Anything that you do for a servant of **GOD** you do for yourself. Anything that you do for a '**GOD HOUSE**' individual who is representative of **GOD**, you do it for yourself and you will be rewarded one million folds plus you will receive indefinite **PROTECTION, MANAGEMENT, INSURANCE** and **SECURITY**. Try **ME** and see!

ENYE ODUDU ABASI MI OOO ZIM ZIM ZIM ASASU POSITIVE POSITIVE POSITIVE !

Some people say things like, 'I have helped people but where is my benefit'? Let **ME** tell you that ninety nine percent of people in the world do **BUSINESS** with Satan. What do you promote in your life? Whatever you promote in your life, you must ask yourself whether it is **POSITIVE**. Are your clothes **POSITIVE**? Is the type of food that you eat **POSITIVE**? Is your name a **POSITIVE** name? Whatever that you stand for is what you promote either it is **POSITIVE** or negative, because you must promote whatever you represent. It is not surprising that people physically promote witchcraft. Instead of people wearing normal clothes that they usually wear, they have now created skeletons as clothes for people to buy and wear. When you promote a skeleton as clothing, it shows that you are promoting negativism and witchcraft which is all evil. Witchcraft is the negative spirit of vampires from the beginning of time from Cain which is from Lucifer's doctrine. These are the people that fight against **LOVE**, **PEACE** and **HARMONY** as such if you promote these things, you are doing **BUSINESS** with evil and you are a **SUPER LOOSER**. If you promote the type of food that is not good, you are a looser. If you promote people that are evil, you are also a looser. If you give loans to evil people and give them money and support them so that you and your evil group will increase, you are a looser. **LOOK, BELIEVE ME or NOT, IT WOULD TAKE ME ONLY ONE SECOND to DESTROY ALL THE EVIL PEOPLE ON EARTH**. I keep quite and have **LONG PATIENCE**, but they continue to promote evil by promoting books that contain the practice of witchcraft and vampire activities and other negative practices that they call stories. You will see the action of what would take place in this world. **I** want people to do **WELL** so that when you are going to perish, you perish **WELL** as it would be the final, final perishing, but **I** want all human beings to know that the final, final **REMEDY** is **LOVE**.

I AM TALKING now so as to reveal all these **REMEDIES** to mankind as the last opportunity, but if you do not adhere and you perish this time, there is no further access to **ME** again and your blood shall be upon you. If you promote negativism, and evil practice, the judgement will follow you, in the spirit, in the soul and in the physical realm and otherwise. When this happens, no one should ask any questions because you know what you are doing and what you are promoting, don't you? Otherwise, practice whatever that you know that is **GOOD** to do, with all your ability and might, and then **I** shall pay you for your effort. You cannot plant cocoyam and expect to harvest plantain. It is exactly what you sow that you shall reap.

You must **PROMOTE THE TRUTH**. If you see **TRUTH** in this **WORD** then **PROMOTE** it. If you see **TRUTH** in King Solomon Spiritual Library as the Library that would help the entire world, then **PROMOTE** it. If you see **POSITIVISM** in the **FATHER'S TALK, EVERLASTING GOSPEL** and in **BROTHERHOOD** of the **CROSS** and **STAR** then you must **PROMOTE** it. If you see any religion that is **POSITIVE** or anybody that is **POSITIVE, PROMOTE** that religion and that person. Do not look at the person's face first on whether he or she is Black or White or whether he or she goes to your church or belongs to your organization. Do not **BELIEVE** in churches, or in an organization rather **BELIEVE** in **TRUTH, LOVE** and **PEACE**. When you know that something is **TRUE** and there is no evil attached to it, then you must **PROMOTE** it and by so doing you stand in the side of **THE FATHER GOD**.

The Lecture Revelation of today is a **NEW BREATH** of **LIFE** as a new **CHANNEL** and **SALVATION** for mankind for the last and very last time. **AFTER THOSE DAYS SAYS THE LORD GOD ALMIGHTY**! If you **PROMOTE GOODNESS, GOODNESS** will follow you. To do **BUSINESS** with **GOD** and to **INVEST** with **THE FATHER GOD THE CREATOR OF THE UNIVERSE** is to hate anything that is evil and **LOVE** anything **GOOD**. Everybody has a conscience and knows what is **POSITIVE**. If you **PROMOTE** the head of Dragon which is a big snake that **I** cursed because it took the system of evil in its template, then it means that you are an animal. If you **PROMOTE** any animal, it means that you are an animal in the human form. However if you **PROMOTE** another man as yourself, that is a human being with **LOVE** then you are **PROMOTING** the image of **GOD** on earth. Every human animal should be a servant to human **GOD**. Animals and all other creations that have been born into this world are angels and they are to serve the real man who is anyone that has **LOVE, PEACE, WISDOM, HUMILITY, MERCY,** and **PATIENCE,** is **EASY TO BE ENTREATED, KIND** and **TRUTHFUL** and resembles **GOD** as a **GOOD** person because **GOD** means **GOOD**. If you see any of these characters in anyone, you should **PROMOTE** that person and worship that person because he or she is **GOD** in the human form.

You should not **PROMOTE** and support those who are fighting, quarrelling and going to war, maltreating people and using craftiness and tricks and all other types of rubbish in an attempt to destroy this world. If you support and **PROMOTE** them to continue to do those things, **I** will place you wherever **I** place them because you are their agent and supporter. Everlasting life belongs to those that **GOD** has blessed. If you **THINK WELL, SPEAK WELL** and **DO WELL** and **LOVE ONE ANOTHER** and **SYNCHRONIZE** yourself away from evil and **SET** yourself with **GOD** and follow all the **POSITIVE** directives around **POSITIVE** behaviour, then link with the right people then you will be **BLESSED**. Select any **POSITIVE** venture and support and **PROMOTE** it. **PROMOTE** what is **GOOD**. **PROMOTE** this **WORD** in cash or kind in accordance with your ability, then **I** will bless you and **PROGRESS** you now and for eternity. Also, if, you are very rich and believe that you are a millionaire, a billionaire, or have trillions then **PROMOTE THE FATHER'S TALK**. And if you think that, you have **WISDOM** and **KNOWLEDGE** and want to **PROGRESS** in life, and in your soul, now, and when you die and come back then **PROMOTE THE FATHER'S TALK**. By so doing you will hold a position of prominence in life. **PROMOTE MY ENCYCLOPAEDIA OF INFINITY** and enable this information to spread all over the world. And as much people that receive **SALVATION** from this **FATHER'S TALK** because of your contribution, then **I** will be rearranging your soul as many times and **I** will also pardon your sin because you have **PROMOTED** what is **GOOD**. **I COMMAND** all **POSITIVE** spirits to **SUPPORT THE POSITIVE WORD**, **THE WORD** of **GOD** and do **BUSINESS** with **THE FATHER GOD** by **INVESTING** with **THE FATHER GOD**. **INVEST** with HRM King Solomon through **MY ENCYCLOPAEDIA OF INFINITY**, King Solomon Spiritual Library and **INVEST** in all **POSITIVE** things. **I** would owe you one million pennies for any penny that you spend **INVESTING** in **THE FATHER'S TALK**. And as you know, **THE FATHER** is **THE SPOKEN WORD** therefore anything that **I** say shall come to pass.

CONCLUSION A: *ONE WITH THE FATHER*

At this stage, you have now become **ONE** with **THE FATHER** and everything will become **FATHER**, **FATHER**, and **FATHER**. **FATHER UNIVERSAL** this and **FATHER UNIVERSAL** that which means that you do not own anything again and that goes for everything that you have including your family and your life. It is only Abraham that really understood **THE FATHER GOD** and that is why **I** made him the Father of the whole world. Both Christians and Muslims and all other religions must join together to believe **THE** same **FATHER** because **I** no longer want division. **I** would reduce any woman that causes division likewise any man or child. Indeed, **I** would reduce anybody that causes division. **I AM** using the name and the blood of

CHRIST to unite the whole world together and that is why **I** have brought **BROTHERHOOD** back as the only way to do that, so that the whole world at large can come back to be one family with the same parent. The only thing that is required from you is to **LOVE YOURSELF** and **ONE ANOTHER**. It is not easy to **LOVE** but if you are able to **LOVE** then you have conquered. Even within the same family as brothers, or sisters or even wife and husband or children, there is misunderstanding but when you **TOLERATE, ENDURE** and **SUCCEED** then you will win the **EVERLASTING** crown as the **STAR** which will endure forever and the whole world would become one. There will no longer be wars because the whole world would become one and that is the meaning of **CROSS** and **STAR** but everyone is automatically **BROTHERHOOD** by nature whether you like it or not because **BROTHERHOOD** means children of the same parent. Are you not 'owo' (human being)? If you are owo then you come from Adam and Eve but if you are not owo then you are a fish, bird or animal and any other creation but it is still **THE FATHER GOD** that created you in the beginning by **THE SPOKEN WORD**. And since the **WORD** is the **CREATOR**, as **THE FATHER** then everything is **ONE** in entity. **THE WORD** created man and lives in man as result man has multiplied into millions all over the world with different names, therefore if you hate anybody, you are a wanted soul. And if you are wicked to any man, you are a wanted soul.

There is no wickedness anymore or bad dreams anymore because **LOVE** reigns and everything is joy, joy, joy on earth from today, now and forevermore, *Amien*. Try and see! From the day, that you become aware of this message and put it into practice by **PROMOTING** and **SUPPORTING** this **WORD** thereby **INVESTING** with **THE FATHER GOD**

THE CREATOR OF THE UNIVERSE, you would not have any bother from any negativism of any kind. If you are sick, you will be **WELL**. If you are poor, you will become **RICH**. If you are low, you will be **HIGH** and even if you are dead, you will come back to **LIVE**. Whatever may be wrong around you, **I** will **MOTIVATE, REMOULD, RENEW**, and **REFURBISH** you, then raise you and **PROMOTE** you for **PROMOTING THE TRUTH** now and forever more, *Amien*.

CONCLUSION B:
THE FIRST CERTIFICATE OF INCORPORATION WAS AWARDED TO ABEL (THE REASON OF KING SOLOMON WEALTH REVEALED)

The first person that did **BUSINESS** with **ME, THE FATHER GOD ALMIGHTY** was Abel. **I** know that many people think that the **WORDS** in the Bible are not true. **MY** dear, if the **WORD** in the Bible is not true then **I AM** now giving you a documented life record. Are you going to tell **ME** that this is also not true? The reason of bringing **THE FATHER'S TALK** was to testify about **THE EVERLASTING GOSPEL** so that for generation upon generations no one should say that it was not a true documented record. This time, all media houses and all Libraries in the whole world would keep copies of **THE FATHER'S TALK**. There will be series of **THE FATHER'S TALK** that would make it last for eternity because it is an **INDEFINITE WORD OF INFINITY**.

Abel was the first person that did **BUSINESS** with **ME** as the first **FAITHFUL** and **TRUSTWORTHY** son. Abel did not have much but when **I** tested him, he passed. **I** said to Abel and Cain that **I** wanted a token of appreciation. Cain brought **ME** food stuff. **I** do not want to go into that today. However, Abel brought the fattest and biggest livestock that he had because he was **TRUTHFUL, FAITHFUL, LOVING**, and a **BELIEVER** of his **FATHER GOD**. Indirectly, that lamb represented Abel's life that he was sacrificing. What did **I** do with that sacrifice as a burnt offering? **I** certainly did not eat it. It was rather a symbol of his heart in terms of how much he appreciated **ME**. **I** was testing him and he passed. As a result, he was the first person that **I** gave a **CERTIFICATE OF INCORPORATION** in **BUSINESS** with **GOD**.

When Abel came back to the world, **I** blessed him as such he came in a big way. Who do you think Joseph was? Joseph was the soul of Abel. Who was Jacob? It was the spirit of the appreciation that Abel showed that **I** used to bless Jacob and it is that appreciation that he passed on to Joseph. When Abel came back physically as King Solomon, he owned everything on earth physically because Abel's death secured all the minerals on earth. **I** secured all the minerals such as crude oil, kerosene, and limestone, gold, silver, cooper, diamonds, aluminium and all other minerals with the blood of Abel whom Cain killed. And that was why the mineral itself became Queen Sheba, the god of the earth as the queendom power. Sheba means wealth and all mundane things as the spirit that controls all wealth and that is why Lucifer attempted to operate through that wealth by using Queen Sheba to control and pollute the world. That is why **I** captured her and put her at the feet of King Solomon because King Solomon owns all the minerals, as Abel therefore he was able to control Queen Sheba. From then till now all the wealth belongs to **ME** in the name of Our Lord Jesus Christ. **I** took Queen Sheba and put her at the feet of King Solomon because she was using her wealth to sponsor Egyptian gods. By bringing her to King Solomon, the arch angel destroyed the temple of queendom for eternity and all wealth now belongs to **THE FATHER GOD THE CREATOR THE UNIVERSE, THE RIGHTFUL OWNER**! And that was why the blood of Abel secured wealth for his **FATHER GOD** for eternity. This is why the three wise men, brought *Frankincense*, *Myrrh* and *Gold*, to honour **ME** when **I** came to the world as **OUR LORD JESUS CHRIST** as the owner of everything. Those three things represent the *wealth*, the *power* and *glory*. This is the reason why you should do **BUSINESS** with **GOD** because without which you are responsible for whatever happens to you.

Abraham did **BUSINESS** with **GOD** but Joseph did not do anything. He simply inherited the goodness of Abel passing on from Jacob. When you hear the statement in the Bible that says Esau **I** hate and Jacob **I LOVE**, it was because of Abel. 'When a child is not yet born', says the prophecy in the Bible 'that the senior shall serve the younger'. And who is the senior child that must serve the younger in this scenario? It is Cain that must serve Abel. And that is the meaning of doing **BUSINESS** with **GOD**. Have you not seen what is happening?

Abraham did **BUSINESS** with **GOD** by giving one tenth of everything that he had to **THE FATHER GOD** and also worshiped **THE FATHER GOD** and to cap that, he offered his son Isaac as a token of appreciation to **GOD** and that meant that he recognized **ME**. From these basis **I** called him **MY** friend and from there **I** made a covenant with Abraham that, he was going to be the Father of all nations and also that through his seed **I** would inherit the world.

You can now see that **I** blessed Abraham, Jacob and Joseph. If you do **BUSINESS** with **ME**, you can never be disappointed. In this world if see that people are very rich, do not judge them because you reap what you sow but if anyone derives their wealth from evil then they would loose it all.

I have given the same blessing to Abel since he came back as King Solomon to reign in his father throne through the same appreciation. For the first time in history, a government on earth, built a temple to signify **THE FATHER GOD'S** dignitary on earth and earmarked the name of **THE FATHER GOD** for eternity. King Solomon used the national purse to do that. Name one head of a country or even a local head that has done this for **GOD** or used the name of **GOD** to rule after David and Solomon in the entire world throughout history and presently. They rather put birds in the back and animals in the front of their emblems. King Solomon had a star as his emblem which represented **LOVE, PEACE, RIGHTEOUSNESS, MERCY** and **KINDNESS** as the five stars which are the five fingers of

GOD to rule. Apart from this, what you see now is snake, lion, dragon and so forth as the emblems of countries. Any country that uses animals as their emblem are a wanted nation and if you read the revelation titled **THE TRUE IDENTITY**, you will know what would follow them for this act. **I AM** keeping quite but **I** will not keep quite forever. You will see what will befall any country that uses the emblem of Lucifer, the emblem of Satan or that of animals as their emblem of worship. Is it those things that control them? Everybody should use human beings as an emblem to represent **THE FATHER GOD THE CREATOR OF THE UNIVERSE**.

CONCLUSION C:
ANYONE THAT DOES BUSINESS WITH ME THE FATHER GOD CAN NEVER FAIL

Children of Israel became number one in the whole world because of the emblem of star blessing of King David and Solomon. What has made United Kingdoms' fiscal value greater that anywhere in the world today? America is very rich because they are sibling of Great Britain, And Americans today are children of Blessed Britain 'the star of David'. They are very rich places in the world, but they cannot compare with the United States and the United Kingdom. The reason for this is because of King James who was the transit spirit of King Solomon who manifested in the United Kingdom to establish charity and assemble the authorised version of the Bible so that **THE WORD OF GOD** would spread all over the world. UK is the home base of missionaries because **I** established it for that purpose and now America has become the Missionaries Home as continuity of Britain. **I** established the United States of America as a United Home Centre to compensate the souls of slavery that was traded by the United Kingdom. Due to all these factors such as having hoped to see the **WORD** of **GOD** manifesting in King Solomon and his charity through King James, the United Kingdom and the United States of America has greater works to do in Africa because they have value than anywhere in the world before now. No matter how other countries are rich, the pound sterling has greater value than any other place in the world because of King Solomon' presence as King James therefore, the wealth has been transit here. However, wait and see what will happen to them if they continue going to war to kill people, they will lose that blessing. Therefore, in a few times to come you will see what will happen in Akwa Ibom State of Nigeria in Africa since **I** have sent King Solomon back there. Before he was born there **I** made a point of burying the wealth that would feed the entire world in Akwa Ibom State and you would hear and see this when the time comes.

The wealth that would be sufficient for the entire world is in where King Solomon was born. And this is why **I** say that you should go back and check the record and you find that anyone that does **BUSINESS** with **GOD** can never fail and can not be poor. Anyone that wants to be great should be a servant. Anyone that wants to be big should be a minister. Spread **THE WORD OF GOD**, **PROMOTE THE FATHER GOD'S BUSINESS** and do **BUSINESS** with **ME THE FATHER GOD** and **INVEST** with **THE FATHER GOD THE CREATOR OF THE UNIVERSE THE RIGHTFUL OWNER OF ALL THINGS** and you will see the benefits to be derived form it. However if you **INVEST** in **PROMOTING** WARS, witchcraft, dragon, and prostitution and all sorts of evil things you will be dammed and have nowhere to go, now and forevermore, *Amien*.

Let **MY** peace and blessing abide with the entire world now and forever more, *Amien*.

In the Name of Our Lord Jesus Christ,
In the Blood of Our Lord Jesus Christ,
Now and forever more, *Amien*.

THANK YOU FATHER

Prayer of thanks by: HRM Queen Disem

Let thanks and praises be given to **THE FATHER** in the name of Our Lord Jesus Christ, *Amien*.
Let thanks and praises be given to **THE FATHER** in the blood of Our Lord Jesus Christ, *Amien*.
Let thanks and praises be given to **THE SUPREME BUSINESS SPIRIT, THE INVESTOR, THE CREATOR OF ALL THINGS** even now and forever, more, *Amien*.

HOLY, HOLY FATHER, thank **YOU** for coming by **THYSELF** to give this lecture through **THY BOUNTIFUL LOVE** for mankind to reveal that all **THY** creation should **INVEST** in thee.

Thank **YOU FATHER** for the spirit of **LOVE**, tolerance and endurance that you have given unto thy children to be able to pass the test of **LOVE** and conquer as you are **THE SUPREME CONQUEROR**.
Thank **YOU FATHER OLUMBA OLUMBA OBU** for the spirit to be able to **INVEST** in what is **GOOD** because **GOOD** is **GOD**. Thank **YOU FATHER** for the ability to **INVEST** in what is **GOOD** which means we **INVEST** in **THE FATHER GOD THE CREATOR OF THE UNIVERSE**, and by us **INVESTING** in what is **GOOD**, we **PROMOTE** what is **GOOD**, and in-turn, **GOOD** will **PROMOTE GOOD**, thereby manifesting **THE GLORY** of **GOD** for all creation now and forevermore, *Amien*.

Let thanks and praises be given to **THE FATHER** in the name of Our Lord Jesus Christ, *Amien*.
Let thanks and praises be given to **THE FATHER** in the blood of Our Lord Jesus Christ, *Amien*.

The Spiritual General Manual Of Life

Let thanks and praises be given to **THE SUPREME BUSINESS PHENOMENON WHOM** has come to establish the **BUSINESS** that can not fail you if you **INVEST** in it, now and forever, more, *Amien.*

THANK YOU FATHER
=========

CHAPTER FOUR

LIFE EXTENSION MANUAL
========
AUTOMATIC SYSTEM OF LIFE RENEWAL

The Spiritual General Manual Of Life

FATHER'S TALK
(GOD PRESENT)

Date: BF/OA/OH Twenty sixth day of the tenth month of **THE FATHER** 'year' two thousand and eight

In the Name of Our Lord Jesus Christ
In the Blood of Our Lord Jesus Christ
Now and forever more, *Amien*.

LIFE EXTENSION MANUAL

A, INTRODUCTION: AUTOMATIC SYSTEM OF LIFE RENEWAL

I have always maintained that **I** would not hide anything from humans since human beings are the image and likeness of **GOD**. From now on till eternity, humans would have the opportunity to learn everything from **THE FATHER GOD** and not from any intermediary spirit. Every human being would learn from the **WORD ITSELF**, the **POSITIVE WORD**.

Every human being on earth that has access to **THE FATHER'S TALK (GOD PRESENT)** and the **EVERLASTING GOSPEL** would know that this **WORD** is for the edification of humankind. It is for helping your inner-self to grow and to be elevated to have the higher consciousness to know **THE FATHER GOD** and to know yourself so that you will know what you are doing. **GOD'S TIME IS THE BEST** and **MY SEASON IS GOOD** and that is the reason that **I** bring all these lectures from the **COMPREHENSIVE MEMORY** and **ABILITY INSTINCT** of HRM King Solomon David Jesse **ETE**. This is to show you that **I** created mankind in **MY** image and likeness. Human person is **MY** city, human person is **MY** temple, human person is **MY** nation, and human person is everything for **ME** and that is why **I** live in every human being to manifest **MYSELF** through the **WORD**. That is why the **WORD** that you are hearing now is not from a mere mind or carnal instinct; it is from **THE SUPREME**

ENERGY OF GOD which is motivating this **WORD** through the **POSSESSING SPIRIT OF ALMIGHTY FATHER GOD INSPIRING HRM** King Solomon **ETE** in all capacities so that this **WORD** would be correct without hindrance for all humankind to benefit. This is the fullness of time. There is no need for analyses in **THE FATHER'S TALK (GOD PRESENT)** and you do not need interpretation. **THE FATHER'S TALK (GOD PRESENT)** is as it is. It means exactly what it says. And **I** will bring different **FATHER'S TALK (GOD PRESENT)** as different Lecture Revelations on all aspects of **LIFE**. You do not need anyone to interpret **THE FATHER TALK (GOD PRESENT)** for you. When you read the information, it is straightforward and direct, and the studio where the information is broadcasted from is that of **THE ALMIGHTY FATHER GOD**. And that is why today's lecture is an automatic system of **LIFE RENEWAL** hence, the title, **LIFE**

EXTENSION MANUAL, THE EXTENSION PROGRAM MANUAL OF LIFE. This is the **MANUAL** that every human soul would use to **EXTEND** their personal life. **I** therefore implore you to bring your heart, your mind, your attention, your faith and believing together because this **WORD** is **POSITIVE**, therefore, you have nothing to lose, nothing to be afraid off and to worry about. All that is required from you is to pay attention and take the **WORD** into your soul and it would give you **LIFE**. It would give **UNDERSTANDING** and **ELEVATE** your spirit which is your inner-self. If you are hungry in your soul, this **WORD** would feed you. This **WORD** is **LIFE ITSELF** and it means that you can **EXTEND YOUR LIFE** from today through this Lecture Revelation. There is no amount of money that would be sufficient to pay for this Lecture Revelation. Nobody on this earth can pay for the title alone with any amount of money or anything on this earth. This Lecture

Revelation is **LIFE** hence the title **LIFE EXTENSION**. The potency that accompanies this Lecture Revelation is **INDEFINITE** in capacity. It works as **WHAT YOU WISH IS WHAT I WISH FOR YOU** so that if you have any problem, of any kind or you face any situation that is negative, such as feeling down, then just read this Lecture Revelation and **BELIEVE** the message. As soon as you read or remember the revelation of **LIFE EXTENSION** then all becomes **INSTANTLY WELL WITH YOU**. You and soul becomes elevated. And that is why **I** implore every soul, be you a human bird, human fish, human animal or human **GOD** or any nature that you are, as long as you can see, read, hear and talk, then you must take this Lecture Revelation very seriously. **GOD'S TIME IS THE BEST** and **MY SEASON IS GOOD** and that is why at this fullness of time, **I** have decided to bring the advance teachings for mankind. You must be serious because there shall be no other teachings again from anyone. The only **ONE** to teach now is **THE FATHER GOD HIMSELF** as **THE SUPER NATURAL TEACHER**, therefore you must utilise this opportunity. All the teachings and information are from **MY** archive record in the spirit manifesting now through King Solomon Spiritual Library. Whether you believe it or not, the **LIFE** of any soul that **BELIEVES** this Lecture Revelation will change in the **POSITIVE** way. It would bring you out from any negative and low estate of life to the **LIFE** where you will enjoy **THE GLORY OF GOD** manifesting in you.

B: **LIFE IN HUMAN**

I have revealed in many Lecture Revelations that every **LIFE** is one **LIFE**. And **I** say again that every **LIFE** is one **LIFE** shared to every soul, therefore **LIFE** means the soul. **LIFE** means **LIGHT** and where there is **LIGHT**, everybody has opportunity to use and enjoy its **BRIGHTNESS**. **LIGHT** shines for every soul equally. Once there is **LIGHT** in a place, everybody uses it and no one can apportion it to individuals by saying certain people should use a little and others use much. A big man would use the **LIGHT** equally as a small person and that is how **GOD** is. **GOD** is **EQUALITY**. If you go to where there is a ceremonial function where there are presidents, head of sates, kings, queens, babies, servants and many other grades of people, you will find that there is **LIGHT** there for everyone to use. Ask yourself this question, is there a portion of **LIGHT** to the king, the queen and a different portion to the baby or the servant or the president? Everybody at that gathering would use the **LIGHT EQUALLY** and that is how **GOD** is. It is human-beings that bring demarcation. It is humans that create different positions and bring differences so that they would make themselves big people. **I, THE**

FATHER GOD, as the **SPOKEN WORD TALKING** now **AM EQUALLY** available to every soul. Whether you are poor or rich, man or woman, adult or child or any other stage of development that you may have reached, **I** pulse **EQUALLY** in everybody. Why should human beings that **I** created who are supposed to be the image and likenesses of **GOD** treat other **LIVES** (people) differently? That is stupidity, and that is what brings misunderstanding, because you do not do things correctly. And that is what **I** call Satan, when you do not do things properly. **I** know that, there are many human persons that are born through the will of **THE FATHER GOD**, and when they hear this lecture, they would re- arrange their minds. **LIFE** means **EQUALITY, LIGHT** means **EQUALITY** and the **WORD** means **EQUALITY**. The **WORD**, the **LIGHT** and the **LIFE** all stand for **EQUALITY. LOVE** also means **EQUALITY**. All of these things that control the existence of **LIFE** mean **EQUALITY** therefore, why should humans try to cave out some positions and portions to show differences. If **GOD** makes you big and keeps you in a particular position, that does not mean that, you are different from another person. A small person dies and a big person lives or a young person dies and an old person lives and vice-versa. Do you not know that **GOD** is not a respecter of anyone? And for that reason, if your senses are working well and you are not sick in your memory and your understanding, then use this **FATHER'S TALK (GOD PRESENT)**, this Lecture Revelation as the **TRUTH** to re-arrange your mind, and treat everybody that comes to your presence **EQUALLY** and that is when you shall have the representation of **GOD** in you. The **LIFE** in a human being means an **EQUAL LIFE** to every soul. It is only when you misuse your **LIFE** that your **LIFE** shortens but through this Lecture Revelation, **I**

AM giving you the opportunity to **EXTEND YOUR LIFE**. This is one of the greatest Lecture Revelations that have come. It is as a result of giving the Lecture Revelation titled **THE MANUAL OF LIFE** that has brought the **LIFE EXTENSION PROGRAM**. If you want your **LIFE** to **EXTEND** from the normal **LIFE**, which **I** have given you, then you must add 'jara', in your conduct. In this context of 'jara' in your conduct, it means that you **EXTEND** the **GOODNESS** of **GOD** to other people through **LOVE**, showing **KINDNESS** and **MERCY**, having **PATIENCE** and making **PEACE** with everyone. When you bear all these **GOOD** fruits, you make people happy and become a benefit to your people and your community and other human beings, just as you will benefit from this **WORD**. And as you benefit from this **WORD**, you would wish that, things should be well for the mouth through which this **WORD** came.

LIFE EXTENSION should be given to the person through whom this **WORD**

is housed, so that he will continue to bring out the **GOOD NEWS** for humankind to benefit. This is how **LIFE EXTENSION** works. A **GOOD** man should live long so that people will continue to enjoy that person. A **POSITIVE** human being should live long so that people would continue to enjoy that person. **LOVE** should continue in your family, so that everybody enjoys it, and that is **LIFE EXTENSION**. Any president, prime minister, king, and queen, church leader, friend, mother, father, child, sister, brother and indeed any human being that is **GOOD** should have **LIFE EXTENSION**, so that people will continue to be **GOOD**, and benefit from such an individual. The reverse is a short life as reduction of life. If any tree does not bear **GOOD** fruit, then, **I** shall cut the life down, and that is '**LIFE REDUCTION**'. This will happen to any president, prime minister; king and queen, church leader, friend, mother, father, child, sister, brother and indeed any human being who is evil, and practices negativism and is not useful to others. If you are supposed to live to be a hundred years of age, you will be lucky to live a quarter of that to see whether you will change. There is no life extension for evil, because evil has no life, evil is hatred and darkness and that means that it is already dead. Darkness has no continuity because **LIGHT** always overcomes darkness. Death has no continuity because whenever **LIFE** arrives it is finished. Poverty has no continuity when **RICHES** arrive because it is finished. This proves to you, that negativism can not exist whenever **POSITIVISM** arrives. Now, **THE FATHER GOD** of **POSITIVISM**, **THE HOLY SPIRIT OF TRUTH, THE POWER**, and **LIFE** is here on earth! **GOODWILL, SUCCESS, GOOD FORTUNE** and all **POSITIVE BLESSINGS** have now established to all **POSITIVE** children of **THE FATHER GOD**, and **I** have **EXTENDED** their **LIFE** for them in spirit, soul, physical truth, and otherwise. When all these blessings of **GOOD** things arrive in your **LIFE**, then your **LIFE** will automatically **EXTEND**. Use this **MANUAL** to guide your personal conducts, because this is how you can **EXTEND** your **LIFE**. Do not exchange people's lives with yours, do not practice life exchange because that is evil, and does not exist. This is **LIFE EXTENSION**, and you have it in your hand. If you want to live long in this world and in your soul, do more **GOOD** things and then these **GOOD** things will **EXTEND** your **LIFE** for you. Have you seen a correct husband that jokes with a **GOOD** wife? Have you seen a correct wife that jokes with their **GOOD** loving husband? Do you see any correct child that jokes with their **GOOD** and loving parents or correct parents that joke with their loving children? A **GOOD** friend does not joke with their **GOOD** friend indeed, when there is any sign of trouble in their relationship, they pray and do everything to sustain it, because that is **LIFE EXTENSION**. **GOODNESS** means **LIFE EXTENSION**. Every situation that is **GOOD** and **POSITIVE** should **AUTOMATICALLY** have **LIFE EXTENSION**. **GOOD** programs, **GOOD** relationships, **GOOD** wealth, every good thing with a **GOOD** spirit, and energy of **POSITIVISM**, should all continue with **LIFE EXTENSION**. If you have wealth and you use it for **GOOD** purposes in helping others, promoting **LOVE**, promoting a **GOOD** programme and promoting any **GOOD** thing that makes **LIFE** enjoyable in a **POSITIVE** way for others, then that wealth should continue and there is **EXTENSION** of **LIFE** for that wealth for you. And any **GOOD** beneficial situation should continue and have **LIFE EXTENSION**. However, if you use your wealth to suppress, deprive and be wicked to people then that wealth will have a reduced life and you will see that, this effect will take place from the day of the Revelation of this Lecture.

LIFE in a human system means that, you should do all manners of **GOOD** things, which would help sustain others in living their **LIFE**, because everybody is a part and parcel of another **LIFE**. It is like electricity wires which connect to each other. From the farm of the electricity station, it is distributed through a **TRANSFORMER** that connects to all consumers and boasted out everywhere. It does not really matter about the distance of the place as long as a wire connects there, then the electricity can be boasted to the place and all can **EQUALLY** use. And this is why you should **EXTEND** the **GOOD LIFE** that you have to people, **EXTEND LOVE, EXTEND PEACE**, and **EXTEND WEALTH** that **GOD** has given you to others. Make sure that you help others to become wealthy, and they would in turn help others. In effect, make sure that your blessing becomes another person's blessing. Your **GOOD** health becomes another person's **GOOD** health. You should **EXTEND** every **GOOD** thing that is in your **POSITION** to another person. However, if it is evil and negative, **I** will shorten it because **I** do not want you to extend any of your evil programmes to other people. **I AM THE ONLY ADA-USONG, (LEADER), THE WORD, THE PEACE** and **EVERYTHING OF EVERYTHING**; therefore, **I** know what **I AM** talking about and **I AM** taking stock now. The distributor of all **GOOD** things is humankind and that is the **LIFE** in every human being, meaning that you must **EXTEND** all **GOOD** things to others, because you have **LIFE**. It is just as you have a child and that child means an **EXTENSION** of your **LIFE**. Anyone that marries becomes two and that means that the two of you have become a **LIFE EXTENSION**, because you will have a child and this child will also have a child and that is how the **LIFE** continues and

EXTENDS in the physical way. That is why if you are **GOOD** then you continue with **GOOD** and if you are evil, you continue with evil. However, **I** have now reduced the evil and negative life to zero and **EXTENDED** all **POSITIVE LIFE** to a **HIGHER CAPACITY**.

C: **GENERAL CONSTRUCTION OF LIFE**

LIFE must be constructed in a **GENERAL** way so that everyone benefits from it. It is about the **GENERAL** concern of the **LIFE** of everyone. Everyone should ask himself or herself about the type of **LIFE** they **LIVE**, in terms of what they have done to benefit another **LIFE** or how they have joined their **LIFE** with another **LIFE**. What **GOOD** thing have you done in your **LIFE** for others to benefit from or have you rather polluted the world? Have you planted a bad seed that would germinate to pollute the environment?

Have you spread a virus of evil life, or have you being a cleanser of **LIFE**? You must be concerned about your **GENERAL LIFE** when you are living on earth, because **GOD** is **THE GENERAL LIFE**. **GOD** is the **LIFE** of spiritual electricity that distributes to the **GENERAL PUBLIC** as well as all living organisms and living creatures, therefore, you are the sub power station to boost that electricity, and give **CURRENT** to people around you, and those people would further give **CURRENT** to those around them. And this would come back to you and that is the meaning of spreading a **POSITIVE LIFE** around for everyone to enjoy. This is what every person should understand and be motivated by in living their **LIFE**. You should be conscious of the fact that, if anyone copies your way of **LIFE**, that person would be not be damned. If someone sees the type of **LIFE** that you live and emulates it, it should make him or her happy and not damn them. Indeed people should comment that there should be a lot of people just like you so that others can copy your pattern of **LIFE**, which is **GOOD**, and when they copy it, it means that a **GOOD** seed is spreading around the environment, which would germinate and make everyone around happy. That is what **I** mean by being concerned about the way that you conduct your **LIFE**. You should think about the type of **LIFE** that you **LIVE** in terms of spreading a **GOOD GENERAL LIFE** to people around. Some people say that there is no **GOD** or they do not believe in **GOD**, but this is a lie, because you believe in **PEACE**, you believe in **LOVE**, you believe in **GOOD LIFE**, you believe in **HARMONY**, you believe in **JOY**, and all **GOOD** things, and that is the meaning of **GOD** and what **LIFE** is about.

D: **HOW TO IMPROVE ONES LIFE**

How do you improve your **LIFE**? Let's say that you have twenty years to live. How would you **IMPROVE** on your **LIFE** by an **EXTENSION** of twenty years or more? Since you have access to this Lecture Revelation and know that you can **EXTEND** your **LIFE**, then you should know what to do to **IMPROVE** your **LIFE**. This is one of the Lecture Revelations that every human being on earth would like to have a copy. Nobody wants to live a short and worthless **LIFE**, physically and in the soul. People, have been doing a lot of things such as practicing of rituals and all sorts of evil things, so that they can exchange their life with another and live long but that is evil and wickedness. However, there is **POSITIVE LIFE EXTENSION** from the **ALMIGHTY SPIRIT. THE SUPREME LIFE HIMSELF** and **I** have given you this opportunity to **EXTEND** your **LIFE** through **ME. I, THE FATHER GOD, THE CREATOR OF THE UNIVERSE** have given you the privilege through **LOVE** and **MERCY** to **EXTEND** your **LIFE** using this **MANUAL**. If you follow this **MANUAL**, and believe in it, and take it as your companion, you can **EXTEND** your **LIFE** in an unlimited form to when you come again in the next generation because, if you can **EXTEND** your **LIFE** now, then you can **EXTEND** it then. You have in your palm, the magic, the potency and the miracle to **EXTEND** your **LIFE**. This is **THE LIFE EXTENSION MANUAL** and within this **MANUAL** there is how to **IMPROVE** your **LIFE**, so as to **EXTEND** it. From today, if you know that you have any hand in negativism, you must voluntarily resign. How do you get away from witchcraft spirit? It is simple, deny the witchcraft and disgrace it openly. Deny it outright and tell all the people that are connected to you in the practice of witchcraft and all negativisms that you are no more with them since you know that you are already dead with them, therefore what is the need to hide instead of confessing. Tell them that you are going to tell the whole world about what they do and from the moment that they hear that, from your mouth, they will not connect you again. You can do this openly and get away from the group of evil because you are already dammed if you don't. Negativism means death and darkness means death. If you have a spirit-soul that enables you go out voluntarily or involuntarily to do wickedness to people and you are proud of it but it is a spirit-soul of witchcraft and all sorts of occultist practice, what do you think will be your end? Satan established those things so that she will have many souls that would perish with her. And that is why such people continue to die everyday and after they have died, they are going to hell fire. They do not die to go to heaven and have **PEACE**. If you read, the Lecture Revelation titled, **THE TRANSFORMER AND TRANSMITTER OF GOD**, *you* will realise that when people die they go to hell. Everybody goes to hell first to pass the test in the hand of Satan before you go to heaven. Heaven means that when you come back on earth you will continue to have an **IMPROVED LIFE**. However, if you stay wherever you are without repentance, you will continue to suffer in the hell. That is hell in three places. Hell in spirit, hell in the soul and hell in the physical life. This is the reason why there is no way that you can escape hell. The only way that you can escape hell and **IMPROVE YOUR LIFE** is to use this **MANUAL OF LIFE EXTENSION** to **EXTEND** your **GOOD LIFE**. If you are evil, you will **EXTEND** your evil punishment with this Lecture Revelation too because everything about **THE FATHER GOD** is in both ways as the opposite and the **ACTUAL** thing as **DIRECT** and indirect, therefore you have the option, but it works according to your **FAITH** and what you **THINK** and what you **WISH**. If you wish to **IMPROVE** your **LIFE**, do not say that it is too late. As long as you are still alive and have access to this information, then you are fortunate therefore you must **CHANGE IMMEDIATELY** and do not waste time. Go on your knees and talk to **THE FATHER GOD** as you are talking to yourself because **I, THE FATHER GOD, AM** a **SPIRIT** and wherever that you are and whatever that you do, **I** see, **I** hear and **I** know. Talk to **ME** as **THE FATHER GOD THE CREATOR OF THE UNIVERSE, THE ONE THAT CREATED** you and also **CREATED** everything that exists as **UNSEEN** and **SEEN, UNHEARD** and **HEARD** and **UNTOUCHABLE** and **TOUCHABLE. TALK** to **ME** as you have made your mind to **CHANGE** from negative to **POSITIVE**. When you speak like that then you should form a witness party and disgrace the evil. What is a witness party? It is to say things openly to the hearing of people about what you have decided to do. If you hide it with you then it will not work. If you have talisman, do not go and throw it away by yourself.

If you throw it away by yourself then it means that, you have done so secretly and it can secretly come back to you. However, if you do it openly and disgrace it then it would never come back. Deny it openly so that it can also deny you. Do you know the amount of quarrelling that a husband and wife or friends always quarrel? A husband and wife can say all sorts of rubbish to each other in their bed but because they do not go outside to do it, they come back and make **PEACE** and nobody hears about it and for that reason, they do not actually break up. However, there is a stage that they can get to where they cannot make that **PEACE** again because they have decided to go up to a point of no return by bringing their dispute into a public arena and that is why if you have decided to leave Satan, do not do it secretly. If you decide to leave evil, do not do it secretly, you must expose their plan so that their plan would not come back to you because it is not you that looks for Satan, it is Satan that looks for you. Satan wants a gang to group for negativism to practice evil and that is what spoils the world. And Satan wants you to have a short **LIFE** and a **LIFE** of destruction so that you will remain in hell. From today, **I** have provided the **MANUAL** of **LIFE EXTENSION** on how to **IMPROVE** your **LIFE** with this Lecture Revelation. After giving you the **MANUAL** of **LIFE**, **I** have now brought the maintenance **MANUAL** on how to live your **LIFE**. You can learn how to **IMPROVE** it, how to **EXTEND** it and how to do it **WELL**.

In the same manner that you practice evil, you must resign form it and you know what **I** mean by evil. For instance, before you become an active witch, other witches and wizards would introduce themselves to you because they do not want you to be a secret witch. They want you to know that you are a real witch and evil and you are involved in incantations and secret cults among other things. They really want you to know what you are involved in because if they use someone unknown to that person, then they would not have any glory on it. However, they have glory on those who have awareness of being their agent as distributors of evil. If you know that you are evil and are in that condition, you must deny it openly. However, you must know that you cannot throw away what you have until you have something else to replace it. You cannot change the environment, but you can remove yourself from that environment and into another one. For this reason, **THE FATHER GOD** becomes your new environment and this **WORD OF GOD** becomes your new environment. **I AM THE FATHER GOD** therefore **I AM** always with you and would not leave you comfortless if you believe in **ME**. **I AM THE HOLY SPIRIT OF TRUTH** and **THE SUPERNATURAL COMFORTER** and **I** would take charge in your **LIFE** immediately you make your decision. Prove yourself to be a changed person which is the actual meaning of becoming born again. It means that you have **IMPROVED**. If you openly deny evil, **I THE FATHER GOD** would also **OPENLY ACCEPT**, and **PROTECT** your soul and you will not have failure. Anything that you hear about demons and evil powers and this and that, all works according to your state of mind and believe. It is a human being that goes about to formulate those things that are said about demons and Satan. When people go about to plan wickedness about you as witches and wizards, they are all human beings. Even the ghost of witch and wizard cannot operate without entering a human being just as **I, THE FATHER GOD** talks through a human being. Without which they would become redundant. There is nothing like evil or Satan. Everything that you hear operates through humans. That is why you must remove yourself completely from the gang of people that you know are wicked people. Separate yourself from darkness and evil because evil works through human beings. If you see an attempt been made on your life in spirit, it is not an abstract spirit operating alone. There is someone somewhere that is planning that. Evil uses people therefore if you have a bad dream, know that someone somewhere is thinking evil about you. Anything that you feel is from the wish of people. Everything on earth is **THE SPIRIT FATHER**, but it is the people that use the negative part and negative mind to be thinking and concocting and using the formula to do evil. You should know that when people go and take things and use it to cover themselves as masquerade by using something to cover their original face so that they can hide to practice something, operate and act, that is the meaning of Satan or **GOD**. That is why if you know that it is a human being that is covered under that masquerade you should call the name of that person and then he or she would not bother you again. This is because that person is trying to hide so that you will think that it is juju (apparition) or masquerade but if you know who that person is say, Akpan, Udoh, Adiaha, James, John, Juliana, Mary, Christiana or whatever be their name and then ask, is that you that is trying to harm me? Once you that, you will find that he or she would stop hiding and remove whatever that they are hiding under.

From today, remove all your pretending coverage as masquerade from your face or **I** will personally expose you. **I** will give a Lecture Revelation titled, **MASQUERADE EXPOSURE** so that you will learn more about this. All the people that cover themselves with masquerades by using birds, snakes and all sorts of things such as other people's faces so that they can go about and practice evil, will be exposed through the above lecture because they are all evil. **GOD** comes with a direct face, apart from in the form of a human being or an angel; you can only see **GOD** as **THE SUPREME LIGHT** which is **POSITIVE**. **GOD** does not cover **HIMSELF**. Today, **I** have given you the method of how to **IMPROVE** your **LIFE** which is to deny evil and join the divine part of **GOD** with **THE HOLY SPIRIT** and use this **LIFE EXTENSION MANUAL** as your guide.

E: **APPRECIATION OF YOUR LIFE EXTENSION, THE PHYSICAL WORD OF YOUR MOUTH AND HEARABLE ABILITY**

When you hear all these Lecture Revelations ranging from **THE MANUAL OF LIFE** and **MANUAL OF THE WORD** among others, including this one, you must promote them. If these Lecture Revelations are **GOOD** for you then make sure that someone else has access to it. If by so doing, anyone reads **THE FATHER'S TALK**

(**GOD PRESENT**) and benefits then you are more blessed. When you make others to benefit, that is the meaning of **LIFE EXTENSION**. It is an **EXTENSION WIRE** in that if you have electricity and your neighbour does not have, then he, she or they are in darkness, therefore you must pass it on to them so that they would also have **LIGHT**. This is what **LIFE** is all about in that by giving to people to benefit from you; you also **IMPROVE** yourself because the person that is benefiting from you will not like to see that you lack **LIGHT**. This person would be thinking well of you and praying that your **LIGHT** does not go off because if your **LIGHT** goes off, then automatically, his or hers would also go off. If you **APPRECIATE** the **WORD** of this **FATHER'S TALK** (**GOD PRESENT**) in all capacities by **THINKING WELL** of it, **SPEAKING WELL** of it, in cash and kind and **APPRECIATE** those involved in its production then you will also continue to benefit form it. You must bless and pray a **GOOD** prayer for the person through whom **I** have used to produce this **LIFE EXTENSION MANUAL** that would bring a **GOOD LIFE** to everyone in the whole universe. For **ME** to bring HRM King Solomon **ETE** into this world as the original King Solomon, it means that, **I** mean well for the entire world. **I** mean well for humankind because **I AM** able to pass through him to give this insight of **ME** so that you will not perish. **I** know that a lot of people understand these things but how many people put it down and even if they put it down, what sort of spirit are they using to bring it out. Even if you were able to deliver this message or are more powerful than this in the negative way, the source of your spirit is not direct from **THE FATHER GOD** because it is not your assignment as such, it would not have any **POWER**. This is not ordinary **WISDOM**; it is the **WISDOM** with **POWER** from the original **SELF** of **GOD**. King Solomon is Abel who became King Solomon of

Israel and now he is King Solomon again. You can see how this is happening unless you do not believe in **ME, THE FATHER GOD THE CREATOR OF THE UNIVERSE**. If you believe that the **WISDOM** of **GOD** means the **DESIGNER** of the whole matter, then, you will know where all these things come from. You should read seven **FATHER'S TALK (GOD PRESENT)** including '**THE TWIN SELF**' and many other things and then pray to **GOD** to reveal where this ability came from as the **COMPREHENSIVE ABILITY MEMORY** that **I** have given to HRM King Solomon **ETE**. Ask whether this is from man or from **GOD ALMIGHTY**. Once you know this then you will know where the ability comes from. You will then understand that reading any of **THE FATHER'S TALK (GOD PRESENT)** is with **THE HOLY SPIRIT** therefore the **LIGHT** of **GOD** will cover you and drive away darkness. If you do not want the **LIGHT** then do not read but as soon as you deny the **LIGHT** more darkness will cover you and that is when you will have shortage of **LIFE**. **SHORTAGE** of **LIFE** means to have shortage of electricity current. Anybody that denies **THE FATHER'S TALK** (**GOD PRESENT**) would have shortage of **LIFE** and shortage of **WORD**. When you have shortage of **WORD** then you will have shortage of **LIFE** because the **WORD** is **LIFE**. And since this **WORD** is **INDEFINITE** as the **INFINITY WORD** of **GOD**, the more you have access to it, the more you **EXTEND** your **LIFE**. The **MORE WORD** that you have the **MORE LIGHT** and the **MORE LIFE**. Do you see that? This is the **TRUTH** about **GOD** therefore show **APPRECIATION** by promoting this **WORD**, in **THINKING WELL, SPEAKING WELL, HEARING WELL** and **DOING WELL**. And what you wish this **FATHER'S TALK** (**GOD PRESENT**) is what **I, THE FATHER GOD** wishes for you. If you wish anybody any evil, then you immediately, wish that evil to your soul because it is the **POWER** of the **WORD** that generates from your **THOUGHT** and your **WORD** before the **EVENT** would take place. You should put together the **WORD** of your thought, the **WORD** of your mouth, and the **WORD** that you hear to **APPRECIATE** the **WORD** of **GOD**. Join HRM King Solomon to **APPRECIATE** the **WORD** season. The first person that **APPRECIATED** the **SPOKEN WORD** on earth was Abel and the second person that **APPRECIATED THE FATHER GOD** was King Solomon by building a temple to earmark the status of **GOD**. And now he has come back to build the **UNIVERSAL SHRINE** to support the **SUPREMACY TEMPLE** which is the **SPOKEN WORD**. And that is why everybody on earth that uses the **WORD** in the **THOUGHT**, to **HEAR** and **SPEAK** must support this program. When you support this program, it amounts to **LIFE EXTENSION** for you because when you **PROMOTE** the **WORD**,

RECOGNIZE the **WORD** and **CELEBRATE** the **WORD**, then you will have **LIFE EXTENSION** and **TROUBLE EXTINGUISHER** in your hand.

F: JOIN THE UNIVERSAL MOVEMENT OF WORD APPRECIATORS

There is going to be so many millions of children of **GOD** that would stand when they hear this program. They would not take advice from their evil parent, preacher, servant, governor or any other evil person. If anybody says that you should not join this movement when the **WORD** is in your **THOUGHT** and the **WORD** is your **SPOKEN COMMUNICATION** and which manifests **EVENTS** for you then such a person is the enemy of the **WORD**. And an enemy of the **WORD** is an enemy of **LIFE** and that means that he or she has prepared himself or herself for **SHORTAGE** of life. However, in the opposite way, if anybody supports you as your **GOOD** mother, your **GOOD** father, you **GOOD** friend, your **GOOD** servant, your **GOOD** governor, your **GOOD** president and any **GOOD** person or personality on earth, in heaven and any other place then they are a friend of the **WORD**.

I, THE FATHER GOD THE CREATOR OF THE UNIVERSE AM so delighted and happy that this program has started on earth. And it is the final, final **SUPREME PROGRAMME** that would **EARMARK, ACKNOWLEDGE** and **APPRECIATE ME, THE FATHER GOD THE CREATOR OF THE UNIVERSE** by **DONATIONS** in **CASH** and **KIND** and in **PRACTICE** by **ACTUALLY CELEBRATING** the **WORD SEASON** for the first time after Abel, and King Solomon. People have been using the **WORD** to get, get, get but nobody ever remembered that the **WORD** is the **MAKER** and the **WORD** is everything as such everybody should **PROMOTE** and

APPRECIATE the **WORD**. And the **TRUE** directive of how to **APPRECIATE** the **WORD** in this world is in the hands of HRM King Solomon David Jesse **ETE**. And if you do it in your own way, it could be that you appreciate Satan because Satan uses the **WORD** and when you do that, you will have shortage of **LIFE**.

APPRECIATING the **WORD** is how you pay for the **SPIRITUAL ELECTRICITY, SPIRITUAL WATER** and the **LIFE** in you. It is the blood, water and the spirit of **LIFE** in you that manifests the **SPOKEN WORD** and that is how you will pay the bill. No amount of money can pay for the bill of your **LIFE** however; you can voluntarily join the group of **APPRECIATORS** on earth directed by HRM King Solomon **ETE** through **THE HOLY SPIRIT OF THE FATHER GOD**.

G: TO BELIEVE THIS INFORMATION AND PRACTICE IT IS LIFE EXTENSION ITSELF

When you **BELIEVE THIS INFORMATION** and this movement and anything about this program, which is **THE SUPREME SEASON OF CELEBRATION TO APPRECIATE THE SPOKEN WORD** then you will have **LIFE EXTENSION**. Once you **BELIEVE** the **MANUAL OF LIFE**, **THE MANUAL OF THE WORD**, **THE MANUAL OF LIFE EXTENSION** and, **INVESTMENT WITH GOD** and all **THE FATHER'S TALK (GOD PRESENT)** as **THE SUPREME WORD OF THE UNIVERSE, THE SUPREME LIGHT**, and **THE SUPREME LOVE** as all together from **THE FATHER GOD THE CREATOR OF THE UNIVERSE**, then you have automatically **EXTENDED** your **LIFE. I AM LIFE** as the **BREATHE** of **LIFE** because when the **BREATHE** of life comes out from you then you die. What is the need of you going to a secret society so that you will have a long **LIFE**? You can have your long **LIFE** from this program through the **MANUAL OF LIFE, MANUAL OF THE SPOKEN WORD, MANUAL OF LIFE EXTENSION** and all **GOOD** things that you do such as promoting this information and building a shrine for it. If you worship this **WORD**, you are not worshiping Satan. If you have access to this information and you worship it, it is better than you worship wood and worship stick and iron or other things. If you worship this **WORD**, you worship **THE FATHER GOD** and if you believe in the **WORD**, you believe in **GOD** and if practice this **WORD**, you practice **GOODNESS**. People have been using the magic of King Solomon and the ring of King Solomon, but now **I** have given the spiritual ring that is **LIFE EXTENSION OF ALL GOOD THINGS** which is *HIDU-CUM* and you must **APPRECIATE** it. Even if you donate one million pounds to support this program, you are not doing much.

You have not even done anything. For you to **PROMOTE LIFE EXTENSION** and have **EXTENSION** of **GOOD HEALTH** and **EXTENSION OF PEACE, EXTENSION** of **GOOD FORTUNE, EXTENSION** of **LIFE** and of **LIFE** to come then you are now **APPRECIATING POSITIVISM** which is **THE FATHER GOD**. If you **APPRECIATE** this program, it means that you deny evil. Anybody that **APPRECIATES** this information and this idea and accepts and believes it has automatically denied all manners of negativisms, voluntarily and taken a new evolution because this is the only way that you can escape damnation. **LIFE EXTENSION** is to **LOVE** one another and that is to **THINK WELL, SPEAK WELL, HEAR WELL** and **DO WELL** and that is the meaning of **LIFE EXTENSION** because it is **GOODWILL EXTENSION**. When you **EXTEND** your **LIFE**, you **EXTEND GOOD LUCK**, you **EXTEND GOOD HEALTH**, you **EXTEND GOOD FORTUNE**, you

EXTEND BLESSINGS, then you will become the **SOURCE** of **LIFE** for others. That is what it is. If you have a stream of water in your house people can come and fetch water there and go and drink. If you have a shop people can come and buy things in your shop. If you have a church people can come and have meetings with you and if you have a big hall people can come and use it for functions and if you have **LIGHT** and people do not have **LIGHT** in their home, they can come tap some **LIGHT** from you. These are all forms of **LIFE EXTENSION**. If you are blessed in your community, you can build a road and when people use that road to enter into their home, that is **LIFE EXTENSION** and any **GOOD** thing that you do is **LIFE EXTENSION** for you. You are **EXTENDING** your **LIFE** through any **GOOD** thing that you do in this world because those who benefit from you will not like you to die, or be sick or to have any problem, therefore you are automatically **EXTENDING** your **LIFE** in all capacities. Will you wish that **I** should not continue to speak this **WORD** through HRM King Solomon David Jesse **ETE**? If you wish him that then, automatically you wish yourself death. That is death in the soul, death in the spirit and death in the physical reality. However, if you wish that **THE FATHER GOD** should continue talking through him to continue to bring more **MANUALS**, more **WORD** of edification and to continue to reveal things through **THE FATHER'S HOLY SPIRIT** that would help the whole <u>world, then you will continue to benefit from your wish</u>. Any day that you join to **CELEBRATE** the **WORD** and thank **GOD** for the **WORD** for making you to be alive to use the **WORD** for **THINKING**, **SPEAKING, HEARING** and taking **DIRECTIVE** and giving **DIRECTIVE**, it means that you are automatically worshiping **THE FATHER GOD** in spirit and in truth. However, you cannot do it in a negative way, you must do it in a **POSITIVE** way by using **LOVE, HUMILITY, PEACE, RIGHTEOUSNESS, KINDNESS, MERCY** and all the **GOOD** virtues of **GOD** to show **APPRECIATION**. This means that automatically you wish that **THE FATHER GOD** should bless HRM King Solomon David Jesse **ETE** and you. If you are not able to do this then you are a child of prediction.

CONCLUSION A:
EVERY HUMAN BEING ON EARTH

EVERY HUMAN BEING ON EARTH has to show **APPRECIATION** to the **WORD**, without exception unless you are not a living soul. If you conceive now, you must ensure that the child would **APPRECIATE** the **WORD** from the moment that he or she is born. All governments and everybody would **APPRECIATE** the **WORD** through **THE UNIVERSAL SUPREME WORD SEASON CELEBRATION**. This is not a matter of my father and mother or my child and this and that has done something so you follow. Everybody has the right because the **LOVE** of **GOD** is for every human being individually not collectively. Since the **LIFE** is in your heart and you use the **WORD** personally, then you must personally **APPRECIATE** the **WORD**. However, if you use it collectively then you must **APPRECIATE** it collectively. In any form that you **APPRECIATE THE FATHER GOD, I** would also give you **EXTENSION OF LIFE** in that capacity. When you see anything happen to you, it means that you have voluntarily decided to give a deaf ear to this instruction of **GOD**. This **WISDOM** and such things have never happened before and this is to show you that what **I** have given to King Solomon, **I** will not give to anybody else. That is why it is through his mouth in today's living world that **I** have revealed this secret that **EVERY HUMAN BEING** has **THOUGHTS**, **SPEAKS**, and **HEARS** and uses the **WORD** to **INSTRUCT** and to take **INSTRUCTION** either by

WRITING, by **SPEAKING**, **HEARING** or by **SIGNING** in any form. Whatever you call yourself whether **GOD** or Satan, it does not matter because **THE WORD** is the **SUPREME ADMINISTRATOR** in heaven on earth. You must individually, collectively or governmentally and otherwise **APPRECIATE** this programme on earth. If you do not do this but you continue to use the **WORD** then you are a debtor and you know what it means to be debtor. **I, THE FATHER GOD THE CREATOR OF THE UNIVERSE** would be **HONOURED** if you heed to this **WORD** through this program. And where will all these gifts go? It would go back to you the **CELEBRANT**, the rich, poor and the needy and to the **WORD** because it is from the **WORD** and it must go back to the **WORD**. **I** have given instructions and directives on how to use all the proceeds that would come through this programme. It is through this that **MY STATUS** as **THE**

CREATOR that all human beings must worship, as **THE FATHER GOD** in **SPIRIT** and in **TRUTH** would become a reality. Do not allow anyone to deceive you because people have been deceiving people for a long time. Arm robbers, politicians, kings and queens, preachers, so called workers of God, workers of idols and sorts of human beings have being benefiting from the **WORD**. They deceive you, yet you build houses for them, you build temples for them and do all sorts of things for them but are they the **WORD**? Are they the **SPOKEN WORD**? However, they are using the **SPOKEN WORD** to command you to do those things. Now his HRM King Solomon David Jesse **ETE** would build a temple for **GOD** called the **SUPREMACY SHRINE**, as the progression of what he built before. It is only in his hands that **I** would accept it. If anyone builds any other thing, that is for small, small gods in the small, small corner. How many cooks should **I** have to cook for **ME**?

Do **I** have to eat from everybody? When you speak to **THE FATHER GOD** individually or collectively, whenever and wherever you are, whether secretly or openly, **I** know about it. **I AM THE WORD** therefore since you are thinking and doing it, **I** would know and **I** would activate your **APPRECIATION IMMEDIATELY**. Try and see and you will realise that when you start doing this you will have right for **LIFE** and **LIFE EXTENSION**. Everybody has a normal **LIFE** for general use, but before you can have a chance of **LIFE EXTENSION** with all amounts of **GOODNESS** that comes with **LIFE** in the **SPIRIT**, **SOUL**, and **PHYSICAL** and **OTHERWISE**, you must **APPRECIATE LIFE** from now on. This is the programme that starts in the eighth year of the everlasting age, the year of the **GLORY OF THE FATHER GOD ALMIGHTY THE CREATOR OF THE UNIVERSE**.

CONCLUSION B:
ONLY ONE MAN TO LEAD ON THIS PROGRAMME

This is **MY** directive therefore do not ask questions. If you ask questions, **I** would know by the **WORD** because it is **THE SPIRIT OF YOUR THOUGHT** that engineers the **SPOKEN WORD**. From there, **I** would know what your motive for asking those questions are. Do you ask why a native doctor collects money and speaks rubbish? Do you ask why a prostitute uses the **WORD** to go about and collect money? Do you ask why the presidents, the governors, the kings and queens, church leaders and other religious leaders and everybody in the whole world uses the **WORD** to collect money? You, that asks these questions, what do you earn from? Without the **WORD**, would you be alive? Will you eat and survive? Is it not the **WORD** that gave you the **LIFE** that you are living now and everything that is in your possession?

Who asks you questions? Why do you want to ask that question now? Why should it be him you ask? It should be you? OK, whatever HRM King Solomon David Jesse **ETE** is, everybody on earth also is. You are the one that would become an **APPRECIATOR** because from the day that you **APPRECIATE**, you can become one of the leaders of this program because when you link with him, he would link you to **ME**. You cannot see **THE FATHER** except through the son. This is the son, the **SPOKEN WORD**, therefore; if you link with this program then you have seen **THE FATHER GOD**. Even if you call yourself Satan, it does mean anything because if you use the **WORD**, then you must **APPRECIATE THE WORD**. If you can think, you must **APPRECIATE** and since you **APPRECIATE** then you are automatically **POSITIVE**.

MY WISDOM SUPERSEDES all wisdom and that is why it is only one man, a servant of **GOD**, the former second **THOUGHT** as Abel is the one that **I** have brought back to the earth, to fulfil this assignment as the greatest assignment on earth. Because he was the first person to **APPRECIATE THE FATHER GOD**, he was proprietor for this program; therefore he must be the one to direct this. As **I** have told you on many occasions, anything that you sow you shall reap. Are you going to argue with **ME** or are you going to say that this is not a **GOOD TRUE** story? Tell me how you came to know that it is not true, and then you blame your heart and your soul. When Abel came, he **APPRECIATED** well and when King Solomon came in the throne of his father King David, he **APPRECIATED GOD** again by the fulfilment of the building of the temple to **EARMARK GOD'S STATUS**. **I** do not live in that building but he built the temple in **MY** name. Show **ME** anyone that is doing that today. Are you not a president that holds all sorts of positions? What do you build? You build churches, mosque, and bethels and build centres for doing all sorts of rubbish and build nuclear weapons that destroy people and cause all sorts of havoc. Who on earth knows that **THE FATHER GOD THAT CREATED HEAVEN AND EARTH**, the **WORD** must be **APPRECIATED**. Did you know that you should be happy and dance in **APPRECIATION** of the **WORD SEASON** and it is for this reason that this Lecture Revelation has come? **I** have waited and waited and nobody has given **ME** the fruit of **MY** labour but today, **I** have come to demand it. And dare you as a human fish, human bird; human animal or human **GOD** refuse to **APPRECIATE**, then you will have shortage of **LIFE** and shortage of **LIFE** means shortage of **WORD**.

CONCLUSION C:
I AM THE WORD AND THE WORD IS THE MAKER OF ALL THINGS.

I want to tell you that the **WORD** you are hearing now is from **THE WORD** that you are hearing now, therefore it is not from another **WORD** to this **WORD**, and it is from the **WORD** to the **WORD**. The **WORD** is the **ONE** that has given this instruction and that **WORD** lives in every human being as the **LIGHT** of every soul. As you are reading or hearing, it means that the **WORD** lives in you but if you do not hear this **WORD** then you will not be blamed. However, through **MY LIFE** of **LIFE**, you can hear this **WORD** from any channel either from a friend, a broadcasting station or any studio that broadcast this information. Any studio that refuses to broadcast this information would have shortage of **LIFE**, shortage of **LIGHT** and shortage of everything because what motivates you to be able broadcast information is the **WORD**.

Any **POSITIVE** way and any **POSITIVE** how that you support this information, you will have **LIFE EXTENSION** to your personal soul and a gathering of your energy therefore this is the instruction that has been given by **THE WORD**, via **THE WORD** and through **THE WORD** which lives in you and every human soul now and forevermore, *Amien*.

Let **MY PEACE** and **BLESSING** abide with the entire world now and forever more, *Amien*.

In the Name of Our Lord Jesus Christ
In the Blood of Our Lord Jesus Christ
Now and forever more, *Amien*.

THANK YOU FATHER
=========

CHAPTER FIVE

LIFE SPIRITUAL FIRE EXTINGUISHER MANUAL

FATHER'S TALK
(GOD PRESENT)

Date: OI/OB/OH: The ninth day of the second month of **THE FATHER** 'year' two thousand and eight

In the Name of Our Lord Jesus Christ
In the Blood of Our Lord Jesus Christ
Now and forever more, *Amien*.

LIFE SPIRITUAL FIRE EXTINGUISHER MANUAL

Today is pleases **ME THE FATHER GOD** to bring this Lecture Revelation titled, **LIFE SPIRITUAL FIRE EXTINGUISHER MANUAL**. The spiritual **FIRE EXTINGUISHER** is **THE UNIVERSAL SUPREME PEACE** that must be imported into every aspect of human life before the **SPIRITUAL FIRE EXTINGUISHER** shall become activated.

A: INTRODUCTION

This Lecture Revelation is to enhance the **LIFE MANUAL, LIFE EXTENSION MANUAL**, but this one comes in a different way because it means, you must guide yourself against evil. Whatever that you see happening physically in this world is the same thing happening in spirit because spirit creates an object soul and an object soul manifest physical reality. And that is from **REAL** to **REALSO** and from **REALSO** to **AMISO**. You should know that due to this **WISDOM** and **UNDERSTANDING** it is only **THE FATHER GOD** that talks like this. *No human being knows this except the PERSON that knows, and the PERSON that does know is the only one that knows how HE does know*. When you say to someone, do you know this and he/she say yes, it is a lie, because you only know what people have told you, but you do not know what you have not created? It is only what you do that you know. Those who create know what they have created; therefore, take this **WORD** of philosophy into your brain, your soul and spirit. It is what you do that you know about, you do not know what you have not done, and if you want to do what you don't know then you do things wrongly. This is why, it is only **THE FATHER GOD** that creates heaven and earth, and also creates all humans that can tell you what to do, and when you do it, it can never be wrong. It is only **THE HOLY SPIRIT OF THE FATHER GOD** that is **TRUTH**, and the reason that only the **HOLY SPIRIT** of **GOD** is **TRUTH** is because, **I** created everything in the whole universe; therefore, **I** know what **I** have done. It is only **ME** in spirit that knows what **I** have put in places. As a result, you do what you do not know and if you think you know, you're wrong. **I** want everybody to use this **MANUAL** because the **LOVE** of **GOD** is sufficient for everybody. It is **THE**

FATHER GOD alone that can bring all these secret Lecture Revelations to help every soul. Some people may know most of these things, because **MY** Holy Spirit inspired many people, **I** reveal a lot of things to many people in this world who are small and uncompleted masters that have come to the world in different ways and **I THE FATHER GOD** lives in them. They communicate with **THE FATHER GOD** and **THE FATHER GOD** communicates with them, but they hide them and keep it to themselves. Some of them do this because of fear of the evil human animals here on earth so they cannot come out openly. They do not practice perfect **LOVE**. In this new arrangement of things, **I** want everybody to be **FREE**. Be in contact with King Solomon Spiritual Library, and then you would be able to explore a lot of information from **THE FATHER GOD**. That is **MY** official Library where **I** have assigned GB (seventy two) million titles of **THE FATHER'S TALK GOD PRESENT** to

HRM King Solomon David Jesse **ETE**. It does not matter when all these things will come out, but **THE FATHER GOD** is working very seriously to bring out a lot of information. **I** know that some people would be asking questions such as, why is it only him, why does **THE FATHER GOD** talk like this through him, and so forth and why does **THE FATHER GOD** talk like this about him? Well read the Lecture Revelation titled, **POSSESSES**. **I AM THE FATHER GOD ALMIGHTY**, and **I** also have **MY** business as human beings also have their business. People copy right, sell formulas and involve in right to sell and rent and so forth, but the original owner of that business is different. You should know that HRM King Solomon David Jesse **ETE** is a virgin in the heart. He is a pure virgin in the heart, a virgin in spirit and virgin in the soul. He has not read books from the world, and he has not joined any secret societies. When he was Abel, and Cain killed him, he did not know anything evil or negative, not even a woman, so when **I** want to deal on **TRUTH** without any problem or any oxymoron spirit, **I** use **MY HOLY SPIRIT** of his soul as the identification **SOUL OF POWER** for the spirit of **TRUTH** for all children of **GOD** which is **PEACE**. This is why you should not ask questions about HRM King Solomon **ETE**, as to whether he is a righteous person, and or whether he is a holy person or he has money or speaks good English, and does this or that. All those things are carnal and mundane things but **MY SPIRIT** in him and the virgin nature that **I** created him with is what matters. There are some of you who have come to the world so many times and done all sorts of things and mixed up so many things. Tell me what a professor in the academia would write if **I** pass through them with this information. They would mix it with their own knowledge from the world. They would mix it with the knowledge of their master's degrees and other stages of their educational level. **I** talk through people everyday, but they mix it with other things. Some of them are fear of speaking the truth, but the one that **I AM** talking through HRM King Solomon David Jesse **ETE** is '**RAW** and **PURE**'. If you want to go and interpret it in your own English, it is up to you and with your evil way, but **I** make sure that the understanding in the **FATHER'S TALK** (**GOD PRESENT**) is there and remains forever in the Name and Blood of Our Lord Jesus Christ. **I AM** therefore establishing **SPIRITUAL LIFE FIRE EXTINGUISHER** for every human being as the **MANUAL** that you can use to live a **PERFECT** and accurate **PEACEFUL LIFE** here on earth.

B: **THE SPIRITUAL FIRE FROM THE SPIRIT OF DARKNESS**

There are so many evil fires burning everywhere in the soul, in the spirit and in the physical human beings causing confusion up and down. Sometimes when **FIRE** burns in a place physically, people would call the fire service to go and put it off, however if that **FIRE** is burning in the spirit, what or who will you call to put it off? Do you not see that fire is burning in every family, home, town, communities, churches, company's houses, and religious groups, all governmental circles, countries and everywhere now? Show **ME** a family that are living in total **PEACE**. Husbands and wives have misunderstanding and are quarrelling up and down, because of the **SPIRITUAL FIRE** of evil. Brothers and sisters, friends, and parents and their children and all sorts of relationships are having difficulties, because of the evil **FIRE** that is burning between them. **Evil** has been burning **FIRES** all over the place. The next person that sits next to you can be evil. There is a lot of practical evils such as soothsayers, demons and all sorts of evil people that have died in sin that are roaming about souls causing **FIRE** to burn and creating confusion everywhere, here and there. How would you escape this problem? These things happen so that you will go to people to find refuge, but the people that you go into are their agents. Satan uses witchcraft to disturb your life, because evil souls of people who die in wickedness are witchcraft and also the vampire spirit soul of Lucifer. It shows itself in masqueraded forms as a dog chasing you or some other animal in the dream and all sorts of things like that. When they do that, they want you to go and consult their agents. Who are their agents? There are some of them who have disguised themselves as preachers, prayer givers, native doctors, medical doctors and so called palm readers among others. So many medical doctors are members of secret societies, members of witchcraft and are therefore agents of Satan. Many native doctors and many people that disguise themselves to have prayer houses or churches, and other places of worship in many religions are working for Satan. They are members of secret societies, they have talismans and they worship elementary spirits soul and practice incantations and sacrifice secretly. All these people that place themselves as helpers in the matters of spiritual or physical difficulties are agents of Satan. As a result, whom are you going to go to for a remedy from all your problems, when you go and consult the same evil agents? Instead, they initiate you and make you one of them. Therefore, from today if you have faith in **ME THE FATHER GOD ALMIGHTY THE SUPREME WORD OF THE UNIVERSE**, you will start right now to communicate direct with **ME** via **WORD**. That thing that they give you to drink is to make you one of them and link you to evil. That thing that they give to you to bury in the ground or to hang some where or on your neck is to link you to evil. The books that you are reading that is written from that inspiration of evil are to link you to evil. Any spoken word that an evil man speaks is to link you to evil, therefore, how are you going to escape from all these things that are causing evil fires? It is through this **LIFE SPIRITUAL FIRE EXTINGUISHER MANUAL** that all evil fire can be quenched. All these things are the evil **FIRES** that burn everywhere, therefore use this **MANUAL** to quench the **FIRE** of evil. Anybody that reads this **MANUAL** and accepts and believes it would surely escape from the evil **FIRE** that burns everywhere.

C: **PUT OFF THE EVIL FIRE WITH THIS MANUAL**

Use this **MANUAL** to put **OFF ALL** evil **FIRES** and all the craftiness of evil. As **I** said above, there is a lot of craftiness in this world. Some governments of this world and some groups of humans have some secret agents that go about making **LIFE** difficult in so many ways for so many people. If you do not join them, they make **LIFE** difficult in so many ways. Some of you join them unknowingly, and when they get hold of you, they do not leave you, therefore how do you escape from evil? You escape from evil, if you believe the **FATHER'S TALK (GOD PRESENT)** in you and you believe **ME** as your **FATHER GOD**, that **I AM** your **CREATOR** and also the one that **CREATED HEAVEN AND EARTH**, then you can escape from all evil. You can escape the evil traps.

Throw the talisman away, burn the membership card of evil secret society and separate yourself away from all forms of negativism. You will not die and nothing will happen to you, but before you do that you must believe in the **SUPREME LOVE** which is **THE FATHER GOD** because **LOVE** has nothing to do with **NEGATIVISM**. You must **LOVE** one another and **THINK WELL, SPEAK WELL, HEAR WELL** and **DO WELL ALL THE TIME** and when you do that, you have signed on to **THE FATHER GOD** and you will have maximum security and join in the **UNIVERSAL GREAT SUPREME WORD SEASON CELEBRATION** with **THE UNIVERSAL SUPREME PEACEMAKER ORGANIZATION (THUNISAL SUPRE-MARON)**. When you do this, you have automatically taken evolution to do away with negativism and stand with the **SUPREME FATHER GOD** that will give you **SUPREME COVER** and **MAXIMUM INSURANCE** and **SECURITY** for **LIFE**. Do not be afraid that evil will kill you. There is a frightening horror like command that evil people give to their members. When they entangle your neck and get you into their system, they will tell you that any day that you leave, they will kill you. And they will tell you that if you confess that you are witch, they will kill you but you have many people confessing everyday that do not die. They only frighten you so that when you shake, you die before your time. You should know that fear is death, therefore, if you fear, you die. If you know that you will die from being part of evil, you will become a frustrated and homeless soul when you die in sin, therefore why not stay here in **LIFE** and deny evil so that when you die as a confessed human being, you take evolution to **POSITIVE GOD**. After this when you die you will go back to **THE FATHER GOD** and **I** will re-house you. **I** will give a Lecture Revelation titled, **HOMELESS SOUL** and that is when you will realise that when you die in sin, you will become a homeless soul that would be commanded and invoked by evil people to be used to go about disturbing other people just as it is been done to you now. What is the meaning of ghost, witchcraft or elementary spirit? They are homeless souls as the people that no longer have access to their destination which is **THE FATHER GOD** as where they came from. When something is **GOOD** and it becomes bad, you take it away from the **GOOD** ones because that bad thing has no where to fix again because you cannot put is back again when it is already bad. When a **GOOD** thing becomes bad, it cannot go back to spoil the other **GOOD** things. As a result, every soul that comes to the world and practices evil and hate people and does not **LOVE ANOTHER**, when you die with that sin, you will become a homeless soul that people command and use for evil deeds. However, that is not what **I AM** saying now. What **I AM** talking about now is this **MANUAL** that you will use to quench all the evil **FIRES** in your **LIFE**. Put off all the evil **FIRES** around your **LIFE**, your wife, your children, your husband, in your work place and anywhere that you are. Use this **MANUAL** to burn all the evil **FIRES** that evil people are burning everywhere.

D: THIS MANUAL IS THE SPIRIT OF PEACE

How do you activate this **MANUAL**? This **MANUAL** is information but there is **POTENCY** in it based on **PEACE**. The first thing that you must do is to practice **PEACE**. Any place that you see trouble, avoid that place. Talk about **PEACE**, sing about **PEACE**, be a **PEACE MAKER** and be **PEACEFUL** in everything that you do and that is the **SUPREME ENERGY** that will help you to quench all the **FIRE**. The **LIFE FIRE EXTINGUISHER** that would make the whole world to be one is **PEACE**. It is not magic; it is not a ring or any object. **I** would give you the Lecture Revelation that represents the power of King Solomon, when the **POSITIVE** higher self of King Solomon brought the **POWER** to King Solomon in the form of a ring, which resulted in his **PEACEFUL CHARACTER**. When you use **POWER** and **FORCE** to do something, you cannot conquer but when you apply **PEACE** that is when you **QUENCH** the **FIRE** of all evils. All husbands, wives, children, parents and brothers and sisters should pray for the spirit of **PEACE** to be activated in you. Since it is **GOD** that created you, you have the portion and instinct of **PEACE** inside you. You go about to join evil causes and forcefully creating confusion and trouble everywhere, but it is only **PEACE** that would enable you to quench the **FIRE OF EVIL IN YOUR LIFE** and in the **LIFE** of all who are connected to you everywhere, here and there. This is why the spirit of **PEACE** is what you need.

E: **THE SIGN OF A TRUE CHILD OF GOD IS PEACE**

Do not allow anybody to deceive you. You can have any name that you like about **GOD** or you can do many things in the name of **GOD** but the only thing that you can really do about **GOD** is to have **PEACE** and be

PEACEFUL. If you have **PEACE**, you will be **PEACEFUL** and that reveals as a child of **GOD**. The true sign of a child of **GOD** is **PEACE** therefore, you must be **PEACEFUL**. When you walk, walk **PEACEFULLY**, when you **SPEAK**, **SPEAK PEACEFULLY** and even in your **THOUGHT**, **THINK PEACEFULLY**. Your eyes should look **PEACEFULLY**, and your hands should touch **PEACEFULLY** and everything that you do should be done **PEACEFULLY**. Be **PEACEFUL** in your work place, be a **PEACEFUL** father, be a **PEACEFUL** mother, be a **PEACEFUL** wife, be a **PEACEFUL** husband and be a **PEACEFUL** child. Be a **PEACEFUL** manger, a **PEACEFUL** teacher, a **PEACEFUL** president, a **PEACEFUL** prime minister, **PEACEFUL** head of state, **PEACEFUL** governor, a **PEACEFUL** chairperson and in all endeavours of work, relationships and activity you must, strife to be **PEACEFUL** and use **PEACE** then you will quench all the

FIRES that want to disturb your **LIFE** and your environment.

F: **TROUBLESOME PEOPLE ARE SATAN INCARNATE**

In the reverse, all troublesome people are Satan incarnate. You may ask what Satan is and what is evil and demon is? It is a troublesome person as someone that speaks without thinking about what they are going to say and whether their **WORD** would bring trouble or someone that walks on the road without thinking about whether their way of life would bring trouble. Someone that drives on the road without thinking whether the way that they drive would cause trouble. Someone that looks without considering whether what they look at would cause trouble. Someone that thinks and does not consider whether what they think will cause trouble. In effect, it is anyone that practices anything without first considering whether what they are going to say or do will cause trouble before embarking on it. You just do things and cause trouble then you become troublesome person then you are presenting Satan, demon and evil. Such a home and such a working place are the vicinities that cannot be **PEACEFUL**, because you are ruling with trouble. A troublesome manager cannot have happy workers. A troublesome director cannot have any happy workers that work for him or her. If you are not a **PEACEFUL** person then you must be a troublesome person. It has to be one way or the other because there are two ways that reveal children of **GOD** and children of Satan as **GOD** incarnate and Satan incarnate. A **PEACEFUL** person is **GOD** incarnate and a troublesome person is Satan incarnate and that is it. Within this **LIFE SPIRITUAL FIRE EXTINGUISHER**, you are now revealed and **I** also reveal who people are because whatever you are, you are revealed in this **LIFE SPIRITUAL**

FIRE EXTINGUISHER and that would work for you according to what you stand for.

G: QUENCH ALL FIRE WITH THE SUPREME SPIRIT OF PEACE

Although **I** will give lecture a titled **THE PEACE MAKER**, this is the **MANUAL of LIFE SPIRITUAL FIRE EXTINGUISHER** that would quench all **FIRES** that burn everyday in human **LIFE**. What causes all the problems in the world? What causes unrest, fighting and killing in the Arab world, Christian world, Asian World and in the Islamic world? What makes a brother and brother fight? Why should Christian and Muslim fight? Why should there be wars in Iraq, in Israel and Palestine and all sorts of places? It is because there is **FIRE** of evil burning in their heart and in their instinct and emotion. Satan is hiding inside them to cause confusion up and down.

When you see any family that are **PEACEFUL** or any work place that is **GOOD**, you will see that Satan would bring a stupid idea that would create confusion. To quench the **FIRE** of evil, use the **SUPREME PEACE** in your **THOUGHT** and behaviour in everything that you do. For any **PEACEFUL** man that does not go to war, war would go to its war and it would not reach you.

Humility is a sign of **PEACE** and if you do not have humility, you will not humble yourself enough to make **PEACE**. Why should you make **PEACE** when you are arrogant? You think that it is like surrounding to your enemy but is not. **LOVE** and **HUMILITY** proceeds glory therefore if you are a **PEACEMAKER** you will inherit the world. The **POWER** of **GOD** lies with a **PEACEMAKER** because if you are not **PEACEFUL** and **GOD** gives you **POWER** then you will destroy people. The mind of **PEACE** is the activator of **LOVE**. If you have

PEACE in your **LIFE, I** mean **SUPREME PEACE**, the **PEACE** that has no beginning and no end and the **PEACE** that is the **HOLY SPIRIT**, then, you must use it. Even though you are not that **PEACE**, you must use the **SPIRIT** of **PEACE**. From today, kneel down talk to **THE FATHER GOD**, by saying **THE FATHER GOD, THE SUPREME SPIRIT OF ALL THINGS, CREATED HEAVEN AND EARTH** whose **POWER** is **UNLIMITED, I** want to have **PEACE** so that wherever I am there would be **PEACE**. When you say this to your soul and **BELIEVE** in **HIM** then you will have **PEACE** because **I** will give you that **PEACE** and you will have the **SPIRIT** of **PEACE**. And from there whenever you are with people that are trying to bring some ideas that are not **PEACEFUL**, deny them, then you will see the sign of **PEACE** and you will see **PEACE** in your **LIFE** and your soul for eternity, in the name of our lord Jesus Christ, *Amien.*

CONCLUSION A: **THE TREE OF LIFE IS PEACE**

When you talk about having access to **THE TREE OF LIFE**, it means **PEACE**. Do you not see how the **WORD** behaves? If you do not use the **WORD** to cause trouble, the **WORD** would never cause trouble. It is what you put in that you take out and that is the **POWER** of the **WORD**. From today, you will use the **POWER** behind the **WORD** in this book titled **LIFE FIRE EXTINGUISHER OF THE SPIRITUAL MANUAL** to conquer all manners of evil so that you can the **TREE** of **LIFE** which is **PEACE**. **THE PRESENCE OF PEACE** is **GOD PRESENT** and that is the **TREE OF LIFE**. Blessed are the **PEACEMAKERS** for they shall be called the children of **GOD**. **THE PEACE** is **THE FATHER GOD HIMSELF** therefore if you are a **PEACE MAKER** and talk about **PEACE** and **THINK** about **PEACE** and drink

PEACE and practice **PEACE** then you have taken an automatic evolution to be a child of **GOD**. A child of **GOD** means that you are in the **TREE OF LIFE** and the **LIFE** is your **FATHER** which is the **SPOKEN WORD OF GOD**.

CONCLUSION B: BEAR THE TREE OF LIFE

When you reach the **TREE OF LIFE**, **PEACE** would implant in your **LIFE** then you must surely bear the fruit of **PEACE** because you have been impregnated by the spirit of **PEACE**. Who impregnated you? **PEACE**! Who are you married to, **PEACE**! Who is your friend? **PEACE**! Who is your father? **PEACE**! Who is your mother? **PEACE**! Who is your husband **PEACE**! Who is your wife? **PEACE**! And who is you child or children, **PEACE** as children of **PEACE** and **PEACEMAKERS** and that would mean that you have no problem because **PEACE** rules the entire world. Let's say that the majority of the family's in the world are **PEACEMAKERS** then who would go to war. Why should there be any recruitment of armies and why should there be deadly weapons and nuclear weapons and all sorts of bullets and bombs because there is trouble everywhere therefore people are afraid. The trouble makers should make contact with other trouble makers and all the countries that are **PEACEFUL** should have nothing to worry about and if any country goes to find trouble with them, then **GOD** will disgrace them. If you go about causing problems and making war with people then one day, war will visit you and you, them and there would be so much war that you will run away! All the countries that go to war are indebted to war and there is a flame of fire awaiting them because you must reap exactly what you sow. And you must pay for all the war that you have created. Wait and see what will happen to all the super countries that always go to war and do not listen to **GOD** and change. Why don't you be a **PEACEMAKER** instead of war mongering all over the place. Have you ever seen anyone in the world able to make **PEACE**? You go to a country to make **PEACE** but in your waist, there are bullets in the car that you drive, there is reviver and a bomb inside. And when you call people to come and make **PEACE**, they know that you are carrying guns so they also come with guns. And as you are carrying guns, it means that Satan has made a **FIRE** in your mind therefore; there cannot be **PEACE** where you are.

PEACE goes to **PEACE** because you can only use water to quench **FIRE** not use **FIRE** to deal with **FIRE**. Have you ever seen that before? It is only this **LIFE SPIRITUAL FIRE EXTINGUISHER MANUAL** that can stop the war in the Middle East and stop the war between Palestine and Israel. It will stop the war between Christians Muslims and stop the war between husbands and wives and stop the war between parents and their children and all misunderstandings. There is **FIRE** of evil burning everywhere on earth because the natural **LOVE** of brethren are waxed old. People shout **PEACE, PEACE,** and **PEACE** but there is trouble everywhere but **I THE FATHER GOD**, the **SUPREME LOVE** and the **SUPREME ENERGY** has brought this **MANUAL TO QUENCH THE FIRE EVERYWHERE**.

If you **APPRECIATE** the **WORD** and **APPRECIATE** this **MANUAL** and believe in it and do what **I** say and you stop war and join **PEACE**, by stopping arrogance and taking on **HUMILITY** then this **MANUAL** shall *'EXTINGUISH ALL EVIL FIRE IN YOUR LIFE'*. Read the *'MANUAL OF THE SPOKEN WORD'*, the *'MANUAL OF LIFE'* and *'INVESTMENT WITH GOD'*. All the instruments that I have given via the **WORD** in terms of information from **THE FATHER GOD** are to help you to have a **PEACEFUL** new world. **THINK WELL, SPEAK WELL** and **DO WELL**.

THE SUPREME FUTURE and the **SUPREME BUDGET OF GOD** that **I** have given to humankind are to help you and nobody can pay for it in monetary terms. However, **I** have given it from **LOVE** so that can use it to live a meaningful **LIFE** on earth. This comes from **THE FATHER GOD** through the testimony bearer of the everlasting new world who is HRM King Solomon **ETE** as the spiritual mind of **GOD**, the unlimited and **COMPREHENSIVE MEMORY OF GOD**. **I** have talked through many people and sent many people as prophets who preach and do many things, but people did not listen. This is the last chance for you to listen to this **WORD** that **I** have brought via **THE HOLY SPIRIT** but if you chose not to listen, then your blood will be upon your hand and that is it. Bear the fruit of **PEACE** all the time and the world will change for **GOOD**.

CONCLUSION C: **ONLY THE PEACEMAKER WOULD LIVE WITH ME**

What **I AM** saying now is not a dream. Whenever you have access to this information in any form, you are in the **PRESENT OF THE FATHER GOD** as the **WORD** that lives in you internally, externally and otherwise. It is the **WORD** that you must believe in otherwise you will find trouble yourself.

You must accept to be a **PEACEMAKER** and accept to join the queue of making **PEACE** and **PEACE** will establish by itself because it is not magic. This is the only way to quench the **FIRE** of evil all over the world. Be a **PEACEMAKER** in your family, your working place, in your religious organization, in your country and in everything that you do. Sign up today to be a **PEACEMAKER**. Even if you are not a **PEACEMAKER** in nature, take evolution to be a **PEACEMAKER**. If you believe from today that you would like the spirit of **PEACE**, then **I** have given you the spirit of **PEACE**. **I** have given the whole world the spirit of **PEACE** and **I** restore **PEACE** in the Middle East through this **LIFE FIRE EXTINGUISHER**. Through this **LIFE FIRE EXTINGUISHER, I** have quenched the **FIRE** that has been burning in-between the Palestinian and the Jews in Israel and all other **FIRES** all over the world. Let all the individuals and governments send this information to the whole world that **I** have quenched the **FIRE** today by using this **LIFE SPIRITUAL FIRE EXTINGUISHER** because Satan is the **FIRE**. When you go to your political meetings and speak a type of **WORD** that is not **PEACEFUL**, you cause **FIRE** to bust. That is the **FIRE** of the soul, the **FIRE** of spirit and **FIRE** through your evil **WORD** and the evil souls of evil people! Do you know what happens in this world when people die during engagement in war? When they come back, they are born as warriors. And that is why you see so many warriors in the world causing **FIRE** and shouting and shooting up and down and these noises cause **FIRES** that cause trouble all over the world. How can you quench them? This is the only way **I THE SUPREME FATHER GOD, THE CREATOR OF THE UNIVERSE** wishes that you use this **MANUAL** as **LIFE SPIRITUAL FIRE EXTINGUISHER** to quench all manners of evil **FIRES** on earth using **PEACE** as **THE SUPREME WATER** that waters all positive natures and quenches all evil **FIRES**. And all is **WELL** with the entire world now and forever, more, *Amien*.

Let **MY PEACE** and **BLESSING** abide with all **POSITIVE** human beings that would use this **MANUAL** to become **PEACEMAKERS** and quench the **FIRE** of evil in the whole world now and forevermore, *Amien*.

THANK YOU FATHER
=========

PART FOUR

THE INSPIRATIONAL WRITER

The Spiritual General Manual Of Life

**KING SOLOMON SPIRITUAL LIBRARY
THE GOD ENCYCLOPAEDIA
WORD OF INFINITY**

**INSPIRATIONAL WRITERS AND READERS OF THE FATHER'S TALK
(GOD PRESENT)
KING SOLOMON SPIRITUAL LIBRARY**

In the name of our Lord Jesus Christ, In the blood of our Lord Jesus Christ, Now and forever more, Amien

(A) REFERENCING THE FATHER'S TALK (GOD PRESENT) IN KING SOLOMON SPIRITUAL LIBRARY

I know that some people will be inspired when they visit King Solomon Spiritual Library website or bookshop, and have access to any of **THE FATHER'S TALK (GOD PRESENT)** information through books, electronics, audio and otherwise and are inspired to write or produce any information through the knowledge that they have gained, they must not fail to reference **THE FATHER'S TALK (GOD PRESENT)** in **King**

Solomon Spiritual Library as the source of your inspirations.

(B) THE WORD OF TRUTH AND THE HOLY SPIRIT PRINCIPLES

Since **THE FATHER'S TALK (GOD PRESENT)** is the direct information from **I THE FATHER GOD ALMIGHTY HIMSELF**, all positive children of **GOD** can be, and will be inspired with this **WORD** because the **WORD** of **THE FATHER GOD, THE CREATOR OF THE UNIVERSE** is a Spiritual Case Study for all souls to improve to have self awareness and a Higherself Consciousness.

When you are inspired and you want to write, make sure that your ideas, principles and concepts are based on the Holy Spirit of Truth without changing the ordinance of the **FATHER'S TALK (GOD PRESENT)**.

(C) THERE SHALL BE CONSEQUENCES THAT WOULD FOLLOW THOSE WHO USE THE MEANING, THE CONCEPTS AND THE PRINCIPLES OF THE FATHER'S TALK (GOD PRESENT) FOR THE PURPOSES OF MISLEADING

Consequences shall follow those who use the meaning, the concepts and the principles of **THE FATHER'S TALK (GOD**

PRESENT) for the purposes of misleading in any manner.

Any Human-God, human-animal, human-bird or human-fish who has access to **THE FATHER'S TALK** (**GOD PRESENT**) through any means, be it via books, electronics, audio and otherwise should know that those words are not the words of human beings. The words are transcribed, proofread and accepted by **ME THE FATHER GOD** as it comes from the **SUPREME STUDIO OF THE ALMIGHTY FATHER GOD HIMSELF**, via **King Solomon Spiritual Library**.

When the signal of the information alerts HRM King Solomon David Jesse **ETE** from **I THE FATHER** through the **COMPREHENSIVE MEMORY OF GOD** in Him, at anytime in the day or at night and anywhere, whether on the road or any public place, he will take note of the title of the Revelation Lectures. Sometimes if the location is conducive, lectures can take place immediately. If the location is not conducive, **I THE FATHER GOD** fixes the time for the full Lecture Revelation to take place. Most of the time, some of the Lecture Revelations take about a week, a month or six months and so on, to deliver when **I THE FATHER GOD** brings it back from **HIS SUPREME MEMORY** to HRM King Solomon **ETE**.

Take note that the information of **THE FATHER'S TALK (GOD PRESENT)** is not preaching, or the giving of sermons or shared discussion. **THE FATHER GOD** calls them "***LECTURE***

The Spiritual General Manual Of Life

REVELATIONS", which is a Spiritual Case Study for humankind to improve and have the Higherself Consciousness about himself or herself and their **CREATOR**.

For this reason, every human being that comes across any of the information of the **FATHER'S TALK** (**GOD PRESENT**) should treat it with utmost and absolute respect and reverence at all times.

HRM King Solomon David Jesse **ETE** is not responsible for **THE FATHER'S TALK (GOD PRESENT)** but **ME, THE FATHER GOD HIMSELF. I, THE ALMIGHTY FATHER** only use Him as a way through, just like a loud speaker from the radio or television receiver.

For this reason, HRM King Solomon David Jesse **ETE** will not be held responsible by anyone who does not understand the contents, the concepts and the principles of **THE FATHER'S TALK (GOD PRESENT)** information in King Solomon Spiritual Library. He will not answer any questions or queries from spirit to soul and the physical truth in connection to the above from the lower mind individuals, persons or groups. However, if you are positive and you have love and are humble, have patience and are peaceful and you want to know and understand more of any part of **THE FATHER'S TALK (GOD PRESENT)**; '**You should use fasting and prayer**' and or if anyone has any questions in good faith, he or she is free to write to HRM King Solomon and **THE FATHER** in him will respond. He will not, and there is no response to any questions, queries and anything negative with the craftiness of the evil minds of humankind.

That is why you should first read seven **FATHER'S TALK (GOD PRESENT)** Lecture Revelations before commenting and

THE FATHER GOD with **HIS SUPREME HOLY SPIRIT OF TRUTH** will bless all those who read and accept this information with good faith through the name and blood of our Lord Jesus Christ, *Amien*.

In the name of our Lord Jesus Christ In the blood of our Lord Jesus Christ Now and forever more, Amen

The Spiritual General Manual Of Life

ESTABLISH MY SPIRITUAL LIBRARY

I THE FATHER GOD ALMIGHTY THE SUPREME WORD OF THE UNIVERSE AM THE SPIRITUAL FOOD TO FEED YOUR SOUL. Therefore, **I** want every family in this world, every home in this world, every office, government offices, monarchies, countries, states, regions, counties, communities, local authority compounds, family homes and everyone and everywhere to collect published copies of **THE EVERLASTING GOSPEL AND THE FATHER'S TALK (GOD PRESENT)** Lectures Revelations of KING SOLOMON SPIRITUAL LIBRARY and establish it physically in your houses. This is so that everybody would have these RECORDS. Go to read the books regularly. Every family should have a Library of **MY INFORMATION CENTRE** for their family members.

Every generation of a particular family should be able to easily go to their family Library of KING SOLOMON SPIRITUAL LIBRARY EVERLASTING GOSPEL and the **FATHER'S TALK (GOD PRESENT) Lectures Revelations** and read the Gospels and Lecture Revelations so that generations upon generations will access their KING SOLOMON SPIRITUAL LIBRARY.

You must all have **THE LIBRARY OF THE FATHER GOD ALMIGHTY** called **KING SOLOMON SPIRITUAL LIBRARY THE FATHER'S TALK (GOD PRESENT) LECTURE REVELATIONS** in your homes and offices. The authorities and individuals concerned must see to that. When you establish your branch of KING SOLOMON SPIRITUAL LIBRARY and have the **EVERLASTING GOSPELS** and the **FATHER'S TALK** (**GOD PRESENT**) Lecture Revelations then that place is blessed and secured. In the name and Blood of Our Lord Jesus Christ, now and forever more, *Amien*.

THANK YOU FATHER

The Spiritual General Manual Of Life

"THEUNISAL-SUREME SEACELION"
The Universal Supreme Season Celebration

=========

"THEUNI-SUREME WORA THECRO-THEUNISE"
The Universal Supreme Word Almighty
The Creator Of The Universe

==================

WWW.COME4WORD.COM

THE OFFICIAL SITE FOR

=============

EVERLASTING

UNIVERSAL ALL WORD SEASON APPRECIATION CEREMONIAL PROGRAM

==========

=

THE UNIVERSAL SUPREME

The Spiritual General Manual Of Life

ALL WORD
SEASON
CELEBRATION
(GOD PRESENT)
SOMETHING MORE THAN
'GOLD'

The Spiritual General Manual Of Life

THE HEART OF ALL MEN IS

WORD

===================

THE WORD IS THE MAKER, THE SOLE ADMINISTRATOR AND THE CREATOR OF THE UNIVERSE THEREFORE, ALL HUMANKIND ON EARTH MUST APPRECIATE THE WORD IN ALL CAPACITIES FOREVER

===============

The Spiritual General Manual Of Life

FROM EVERY OA OF AO TO AO OF AO (1ˢᵗ OCTOBER TO 10th OCTOBER). YEARLY IS THE UNIVERSAL SUPREME **ALL WORD SEASON** CELEBRATION TO APPRECIATE THE FATHER GOD ALMIGHTY
==================
CELEBRATION! CELEBRATION!! **CELEBRATION!!**

The Spiritual General Manual Of Life

THE UNIVERSAL SUPREME WORD CELEBRATION OF ALL TIME
=======

The Spiritual General Manual Of Life

THE ALMIGHTY FATHER GOD, THE CREATOR OF ALL

The Spiritual General Manual Of Life

THINGS BROTHERHOOD

ORGANISED BY
KING SOLOMON SPIRITUAL LIBRARY

=======

HRM KING SOLOMON DAVID JESSE ETE
INSPIRATIONAL HEAD

IN THE HONOUR OF THE FATHER GOD THE CREATOR OF THE UNIVERSE THE HOLY SPIRIT OF TRUTH AND THE KING OF KINGS AND THE LORD OF LORDS

===========

The Spiritual General Manual Of Life

THANK YOU FATHER

KING SOLOMON SPIRITUAL LIBRARY

THE GOD ENCYCLOPAEDIA WORD OF INFINITY

============

King Solomon Spiritual Library, God Universal Information Centre
FATHER'S TALK (GOD PRESENT)

WITH LOVE

Covered: **This BOOK,** e-book, software or software's, books, websites, videos, audios, idea or ideas, formula or formulas, manual or instruction manual

... Hereby gives you a non-exclusive license to use the ... (THIS BOOK).

Some of the words here are coded with the (WORD OF SUPER HOLY AND INTELLIGENCE FATHER GOD ALMIGHTY)

Title, ownership rights, and intellectual property rights in and to the Website, Books, E-book, Audios and Videos, Shops and Store – e-Stores, Fundraisings, Celebrations and the Supreme Word Seasons Celebration formulas and arrangements, Positive

Inspiration, HOLY (FATA), FATHER GOD ALMIGHTY POSSESSING SPIRIT in thought, in words and in deed, thinking well, speaking well, hearing well and doing well shall remain in me and in ... The BOOK is protected by international copyright.

FATHER'S TALK (GOD PRESENT)
   The message in **THE FATHER'S TALK (GOD PRESENT)** does not challenge any authority either individuals, groups or governments of any land or even any belief of any form. It is rather challenging the truth that is hidden from mankind. Therefore, any spirit, soul or physical human being who decides to challenge this truth shall have himself or herself to blame.

   Key A

Any individual that reads any of **THE FATHER'S TALK** (GOD PRESENT) with faith; love and acceptance will experience immediate positive change in his or her life from spirit, soul to physical. If he or she accepts the message then he or she will be free from any evil.

Key B: **PEACE AND LOVE**
If you do not believe the contents of any of **THE FATHER'S TALK (GOD PRESENT)**, it is possible through **THE FATHER'S** divine love and peace to simply hand over your copy to a friend or somebody else that would like to keep a copy, or by signing out from any of the websites that connect to **THE FATHER'S TALK (GOD PRESENT)** and KING SOLOMON SPIRITUAL e-LIBRARY

without any evil and negative comments then you are blessed and free.

========

FROM THE DESK OF INSPIRATIONAL HEAD
Fees, Prices and Donations; There is no refund on fees, prices or donations since your fees, prices or donations are used as a charity contribution to do administrative work of **THE SUPREME WORD**, so please kindly read this first before you decide to involve yourself in any of the under mentioned of HRM King Solomon David Jesse **ETE** universal Inspirational Businesses of (**GOD PRESENT**) in cash, kind and otherwise.

I CAME FROM THE FATHER GOD, WITH THE FATHER GOD, AND BY THE FATHER GOD TO ESTABLISH THE FOLLOWING:

All distributors and contributors of **THE FATHER'S TALK** (GOD PRESENT), The Spiritual Advice, Healing and Counselling on General Live (The Universal Supreme Spiritual General Hospital), New Songs and Psalms of King David and Solomon, The Word of **GOD** Processing City in Ikot Okwo or e-City online, The Trinity Celebration, "**OUC FUND**", The Universal Bank Account For All Creations, "**ERUFA**" ETE Royal Universal Family, "**THEUNISAL-SUREME SEACELION**" The Universal Supreme Word Season Celebration To Appreciate **THE FATHER GOD ALMIGHTY "THEUNI-SUREME WORA THECRO-THEUNISE"** The **Universal Supreme Word Almighty**, **THE CREATOR OF THE UNIVERSE** should attach this information to all readers, website visitors, distributors, affiliates person/group, celebrant and celebrations centres, supporters and promoters, members, workers and voluntary workers, Ete royal universal palace committee, governments and many other centres as an agreement. Please kindly know that I am not answering to any physical human except **PEACE, UNITY AND LOVE.**

"THEUNISAL-SUREME WORA THECRO-THEUNISE".

I AM IN THE STAGE OF SUPER HOLY AND INTELLIGENT FATHER GOD POSITIVE MADNESS OF THE HOLY SPIRIT OF TRUTH, ENYEN ODUDU ODUDU ODUDU ABASI MI OOO ZIM ZIM ZIM ASSASU, POSITIVE POSITIVE

POSITIVE. UKEMEKE AKA IDIOK UNAM.

Let the peace and blessing of THE HOLY FATHER abide with everybody who corporates with this divine **FATHER'S TALK (GOD PRESENT)**

THANK YOU FATHER
BY
THE HOLY SPIRIT OF
THE FATHER GOD
THROUGH HIS SERVANT
The Senior Christ Servant
HRM King Solomon David Jesse **ETE**
Brotherhood of the
Cross and STAR
Eteroyal Universal family
Ikot Okwo The Great City of Refuge,
Ete Community
Ikot Abasi LGA-543001
Akwa Ibom State Nigeria-W/A
Tel. 08036693841
Email: ksslibrary@eteroyalmail.com

==============

READ AT LEAST SEVEN LECTURE REVELATIONS BEFORE YOU CAN MAKE ANY COMMENTS

In the Name of Our Lord Jesus Christ, In the Blood of Our Lord Jesus Christ, Now and forever more

Everybody should have access to and read at least seven **FATHER'S TALK**

(**GOD PRESENT**) Lecture Revelations before making any comments about it. If you do not go through at least seven **FATHER'S TALK** Lecture Revelation and you comment, you may make mistakes. And when you make mistakes your blood will be upon you because you would have taken voluntary evolution to misquote **THE FATHER GOD THE CREATOR OF THE UNIVERSE**.

One of **THE FATHER'S TALK** stands for one SPIRIT of GOD, which means that THE **FATHER'S TALK (GOD PRESENT)** Lecture Revelations are witnessed by the Seven SPIRITS of GOD, which **I** use as the Seven Churches of GOD and Seven days of the Week, Seven spirits of Creation in one Supreme energy of **THE FATHER GOD**,
   THE SPOKEN WORD therefore,
   when you read seven **FATHER'S TALK (GOD PRESENT)** Lecture **Revelations** then, **I, THE FATHER GOD** will reveal you as a positive person and then you will have a portion in **ME**. And one of **THE FATHER'S TALK (GOD PRESENT)** will have a portion in you. Then you would know that this information came from **THE FATHER GOD. THE FATHER'S**

TALK (GOD PRESENT) is not a mere talk from a man!
 In the Name of Our Lord Jesus Christ, In the Blood of Our Lord Jesus Christ, Now and forever more

INVITATION
====
THE UNIVERSAL SUPREME ACKNOWLEDGEMENT
'THE ONLY SOURCE AND REMEDY

TO END ALL HUMANITY PROBLEMS'
Join me to Celebrate;
Acknowledge,
Appreciate and give full RECOGNITION to
THE UNIVERSAL SUPREME WORD,
YOUR LIFE FORCE,
THE TOTALITY OF ALL TOTALITIES
YOUR CREATOR,
THE FATHER GOD ALMIGHTY,
THE CREATOR OF THE UNIVERSE

WWW.COME4WORD.COM

The Spiritual General Manual Of Life

Contact EMAIL:
hrmkingsolomon@eteroyalmail.com

THANK YOU FATHER

The title List of some of the

FATHER'S TALK
(GOD PRESENT)

1: THE MANUAL OF THE SPOKEN WORD

2: THE MANUAL OF LIFE

3: INVESTMENT WITH GOD

4: ISO IBOT EDEM IBOT

5: THE CHARACTER OF THE NEW WORLD

6: HELPMANTRANS

7: UNDERSTANDING MY WORD

8: TRUTH, POSITION, POST AND NAME

9: NON STOP BLESSING

10: IMPRESSION

11: STAGES OF EDUCATIONS (SPE, SSE & SUE)

12: THE ENGINEERING OF LIFE

13: THE CONTENT PACKAGE

14: THE BUDGET OF THE NEW WORLD

15: DIVINE ATTENTION

16: THE BABY SPIRIT

17: PROMOTION

18: ADVANCE AND PROGRESSING MIND

19: THE TEMPLE OF THE LIVING GOD

20: I AM OK

21: THE SPIRIT OF TRUTH

22: THE PERFECT PERMANENCY

23: THE FATHER GOD, GOD, GOD THE FATHER

24: HUSBAND, WIFE AND CHILD

25: GOD AND HIS HARBINGER

26: LIFE EVERLASTING

27: POSSESS

28: MY MIND AND MY PLAN

29: AFTER HEART AND AFTER MIND

30: MY DECLARATION & STAND IN BCS

31: BEYOND THE HOPE OF FAITH

32: MENTAL STAIN

33: THE PRINCIPLE OF SELF HOLD

34: THE MASTERSHIP

35: HIDU-CUM

36: THE UNIVERSAL PARENT

37: ADVANCED YOU AND ME

38: THE GREAT UNIVERSAL CHANGE

39: THE PROJECTED MIND
40: INDESTRUCTIBLE BLESSED FIVE STARS

41: ASTROTS, GOD PRESENT I AND MY FATHER

42: SONGS THE COMPLETION

43: THE RIGHT BUTTON

44: AKWA ABASI IBOM- ETE - DIRECTING NDITO AKWA IBOM

45: THE DIGITAL AGE

46: GOD IS OFFICIAL CHAMPION

47: A TRUE WITNESS

48: MYSTERY OF PROCREATION AND BIRTH

49: THE UNIVERSAL UMBRELLA

50: THE FORERUNNER

51: A OF A TO Z (FIRST OF ALL)

52: MAN IN THREE CAPACITIES

53: THE TRUE LIFE OF HOLY SPIRIT PERSONIFIED

54: IN-BETWEEN THE FATHER & THE SON

55: DIVINE ARRANGEMENT & AUTHORITY

56: TWENTY FIRST CENTURY IS NOT FOR SATAN

57: THE SUPREME WORD SEASON CELEBRATION

58: THE MAXIMUM DEITY

59: TRANSFORMER TRANSMITTER AND WAVE

60: THE SUPREME FUTURE

61: THE BYLOVE OF WORD

62: THE SIGNATURE OF THE FATHER GOD

63: THE TWO WAYS

64: THE UNDERSTANDING OF LIFE

65: THE GREATER THAN SOLOMON IS HERE

66: THE CONQUEROR

67: THE SPIRITUAL GENERAL INSPECTOR OF LIFE

**68: THE NIGERIA IN THE AFRICA
Part one**

69: THE NIGERIA IN THE AFRICA
Part two

70: THE CREATOR AND CREATIONS PART ONE

71: THE CREATOR AND CREATIONS PART TWO

72: THE CREATOR AND CREATIONS PART THREE

73: THE SUPREME TEACHER

74: THE SPIRITUAL COVER

75: THE NIGERIA IN THE AFRICA PART THREE

76: THE SUPREME BELIEVE

77: CAST AND BAN (LECTURE IN LIVERPOOL)

78: <u>LIFE EXTENSION MANUAL</u>

79: THE SPIRITUAL TRAFFIC

80: THE VOICE OF THE CREATOR

81: MY OFFICE

82: **LIFE SPIRITUAL FIRE EXTINGUISHER**

83: INFORMATION

84: FATHER GOD FINAL ARRANGEMENT

85: THE LOVERS OF CHRIST

86: I LOVE YOU, I LOVE YOU TOO

87: THE UNIVERSAL SUPREME UPDATE

88: THE SUPREME ALTAR

89: THE SOURCE AND DESTINATION

90: A SON LIKE THE FATHER THE KING OF KINGS A ROOTS FROM HEAVEN (NOT THIS TIME AROUND)

91: THE TRUE WITNESS AND THE TRUE SERVANT

92: THE FINAL ARRANGEMENT

93: A TRUE NIGERIAN MAN AND WOMAN

94: EVERYONE MUST PERSONALLY INVOLVE

95: BEWARE

96: ESIEN EMANA AKPAN "THE AFRICAN PROBLEMS"

97: THE SECRET OF THE UNIVERSAL PROBLEMS AND THE REMEDY (MUSLIM AND CHRISTIAN FROM THE SAME PARENT)

98: MMU-UDIM – THE BLESSED MOTHER (ABASI ME UDIM)

99: THINK WELL, SPEAK WELL AND DO WELL

100: THE STAGES OF HOW TO PROCESS THE WORD

101: EVIL STAIN, WHO RUNS AWAY FROM WHO

102: BEYOND HUMAN KNOW PURELY SPIRITUAL

103: THE INSPIRATIONAL WRITER

104: BIAKPAN OBIO AKPAN ABASI (THE NEW JERUSALEM CITY)

105: "OBAMA" THE STRAINTHEN AND THE SPIRIT OF BILL GATE AND MICOSOFT

THANK YOU FATHER

www.ingramcontent.com/pod-product-compliance
Ingram Content Group UK Ltd.
Pitfield, Milton Keynes, MK11 3LW, UK
UKHW041258180426
11947UKWH00008B/552